Under the Gaze
Learning to Be Black in White Society

Jennifer Kelly

Fernwood Publishing • Halifax

Editing: Anne Webb
Cover photo: George Bernard Jr.
Printed and bound in Canada by: Hignell Printing Limited

second printing 2005

A publication of:
Fernwood Publishing
Site 2A, Box 5, 32 Oceanvista Lane
Black Point, Nova Scotia, B0J 1B0
and 324 Clare Avenue
Winnipeg, Manitoba, R3L 1S3
www.fernwoodbooks.ca

Fernwood Publishing Company Limited gratefully acknowledges the financial support of the Department of Canadian Heritage, the Nova Scotia Department of Tourism and Culture and the Canada Council for the Arts for our publishing program. ▮◆▮ Canadian Patrimoine   The Canada Council for the Arts   NOVA SCOTIA
                           Heritage canadien   Le Conseil des Arts du Canada   Tourism and Culture

Photos reproduced from: Carter, V. and Carter, L. 1990. *The Window of Our Memories Volume II.* Black Cultural Research Society of Alberta.
Carter, V. and Akili, W. 1981. *The Window of Our Memories.* Black Cultural Research Society of Alberta.
City of Edmonton Archives.

Canadian Cataloguing in Publication Data

Kelly, Jennifer.

Under the gaze

Includes bibliographical references.
ISBN 1-895686-2-1

1. Black Canadian students -- Social conditions.* I. Title.

FC106.B6.K44 1998   371.829'96071   C98-950002-0   F1035.N3K44 1998

CONTENTS

Acknowledgements

This book was written during the summer of 1997 in the sunny/rainy climes of Alberta. I would like to thank my three children, Rosa, Clara and Leon, who spent much of their school holidays patiently wondering when I would be finished. I would like to thank my partner, Bruce, who read drafts and listened to me while I wrestled with various ways of tackling this book.

Thanks to my mother Phyllis in Jamaica, for allowing me the freedom in my life to become who I am today. Thanks also to the remainder of my family—here, there and everywhere.

I would like to thank Ann-Marie Decore and Ray Morrow for their academic support and for allowing me time in my academic schedule to complete this book. As well, thanks to Toh Swee-Hin for his patience during the early stages of this project, and to Judy L'Amour, a history tutor with Athabasca University (a telephone tutor—we have never met), for her patience and willingness to listen to my questions during my first educational experience in Canada. I have not forgotten.

Thanks to all the friends I have met in the corridors of life, especially Sue Brigham, Gloria Filax, Donna Chovanec, Hector Gonzalez and Gordon Sidool and Friends in Club IDC. Also, thanks to Rosetta Khalideen who dragged me out on many occasions for a much needed "chat," and to Hijin Park and Yoke-Sum Wong for all those articles to read!

A very special thank-you goes to Malcolm Azania for his willing help in moderating the male focus group, for reading earlier drafts and for his friendship.

Thanks to Stephen Bowen, Meaghan Ellis, Kelly Fraser, Charlene Gentles and Richard Russell who read and commented on this manuscript. And thanks go to Carl James and Carolyn Alyward for reviewing and commenting on earlier drafts.

Thanks to the teachers who took time out of their busy schedules to share their insights—especially Rosalind Smith.

Without a doubt the students who contributed to this project get the biggest thank-you since in many ways this is their book. Without their time, patience, sharp critique and insights this project would not have been accessible.

Among the Fernwood staff, I would like to acknowledge Wayne Antony who received the first proposal for this book with enthusiasm, read drafts and steered its development from manuscript to book. Recognition goes to Anne Webb for the tremendous time and effort she put into the careful editing of the manuscript, to Beverley Rach for production and layout, to Donna Davis for proofreading and to Debbie Mathers for typing.

Chapter One

Introduction
Part I: Researching Race

Jennifer Kelly: *What do Black people have in common with one another?*

Toni: *Experiences with the White man.*

Lorraine: *We've all been there.*

Toni and Lorraine's[1] responses to my question provide a context for the discussion of Black identity undertaken in this book. Although African Canadians come from disparate geographic locations and cultures and hold many different worldviews, they all share the experience of being Black in a White-dominated society. This book illustrates how a specific group of young African Canadians living in Edmonton, Alberta, socially construct themselves as "Blacks." This process of construction is often relational with the youths defining themselves in reference to other social groups. Although their schools provide the common reference point for their experiences recorded in this book, the youths' narratives reveal the complexity of their lives and the role of other social and community influences, including popular culture.

This book demonstrates how *racialization* (giving raced meanings to social situations) takes place in the lives of young Black students. It demonstrates the intricacies of forming a Black *identity*—"an individual's sense of uniqueness, knowing who one is, and who one is not" (Harris 1995: 1)—within a White-dominated society. I do not set out to answer one question or begin with a simple thesis statement. My purpose here is to investigate:

- how Black students view and perceive themselves;
- how they relate to their peers;
- the significance they attach to being "Black" in a White-dominated environment;
- how they receive and perceive predominantly Western popular cultural forms; and

- how they relate to teachers and school.

The first four issues are the major focus of this text. These dynamics are set in a cultural and—in Chapter Two—a historical discussion of the impact of racialization in Canadian society on education, immigration, employment and the armed forces. How the students' identification intersects with their schooling is the focus of the final chapter.

The students' narratives reveal a process of *cultural reproduction*—a process in which a social formation is reproduced into the future via meanings and sense-making. The narratives show how raced meanings get passed on from generation to generation. Cultural reproduction is linked to the identity formation of the students as individuals and as a group as they make sense of, adopt and adapt the different raced meanings that they encounter in society. Identity formation and the adoption of popular forms is revealed in the instances in which the students differentiate themselves from, and associate with, those who are perceived as Black.

The narratives of the students are of course based on their own interactions within society. Their personal experiences are presented here against a background of social, political and historical factors. Contextualizing the personal in this way illustrates the socially constructed nature and meaning of growing up Black in a society dominated historically and intellectually by White Eurocentric culture, that is, in a society where Europe is used as the universal in terms of values, culture and knowledge creation.

For these African Canadian youths, the process of growing up in a White-dominated society can be seen as a process of being *othered*—of being put outside of the dominant group. As part of this othering process African Canadian youths testify that even when they are Canadian-born, they are represented by the dominant culture as not "belonging," as not "really" Canadian. Marlene Nourbese Philip, an African Canadian essayist, sums up this process succinctly:

> Being born elsewhere, having been fashioned in a different cul-
> ture, some of us may always feel "othered," but then there are
> those—our children, nephews, nieces, grandchildren—born here,
> who are as Canadian as snow and ice, and yet, merely because of
> their darker skins, are made to feel "othered." (Philip 1992: 16)

Incidents of othering are illustrated by the narratives of these youths who are growing up in a city on the Prairies where African Canadians are estimated to make up less than 2 percent of the local population. This book reveals how othering affects the way that these youths socialize and interact with their peers, and how they discuss at school the popular culture they perceive and experience.

When discussing "Blackness," identity and culture, it is useful to engage a multidisciplinary approach that is grounded in cultural theory. Much work on identity has tended to focus on the interaction between immigrant and host communities, a focus that is fraught with Eurocentric assumptions about "contact," "assimilation" and "fusion" of the immigrant experience. Thus, discussion of issues of identity benefit from a radical critique of the taken-for-granted meanings of concepts such as culture, race, nation and Black, linked to an analysis of issues relating to power and dominance. The approaches of theorists such as Stuart Hall, Himani Bannerji, bell hooks and Paul Gilroy[2] open up for discussion the process of racialization and how it affects the formation of a Black identity. This book offers a critique of the positioning of the individual and society as separate from each other. It attempts to move away from psychological accounts that place the rational, all-knowing individual at the centre of human action. Building on the work of the cultural theorists above, the book offers a sense of identity that is complex and layered. In some ways, the book replaces "human nature with the concepts of history, society and culture as determining factors in the construction of identity" and further "destabilizes that identity by making it an effect rather than simply an origin of linguistic practice" (Easthope and McGowan 1992: 67).

Terminology and Categories

The terminology used when discussing and researching race is problematic, contentious and ambiguous. Often this is because the use of certain terms becomes part of a power struggle between groups in society. For example, what is meant by the term Black and who should be included within a group defined as Black? The data collection undertaken by Statistics Canada is an illustration of the way in which concrete problems result from theoretical ambiguity and confusion in categorization. Use of categories such as "Black origins" and "Caribbean origins" in census questionnaires lead to multiple and inconsistent responses, which makes differentiation and analysis of different population groups difficult.

Recent findings by the McGill Consortium for Ethnicity and Strategic Social Planning (Torczyner 1997) also illustrate the complexities surrounding the gathering and consequent use of census data and the categorization of Black Canadians. Using a more inclusive grouping than the restrictive Statistics Canada identification, which is based on a single component of identity, the McGill Consortium has come up with "more than twice the 'pure' count of reported Black origins" (Torczyner 1997: 11).[3] Thus, by revising the categorization used in the 1991 census, the consortium estimates that the Black population in Edmonton is about 1.4 percent of the total city population, an upwards revision from 7,000 to 11,745. The 1996 census was designed to eliminate some of this ambiguity through the addition of a direct question on race, but there was much controversy as to whether there was such a thing as race and if people should still see themselves in such terms. The latter controversy highlights not only the importance of self-categorization, but also the reality that our self-categorization might not coincide with how others categorize us. This disjuncture is an issue of discussion among those of us of African descent, as some of us re-categorize ourselves as African Canadians rather than Black in recognition of our roots in Africa. How does the variance in categorization impact the political rationale for "programmes that promote equal opportunity for everyone to share in the social, cultural and economic life of Canada" (Statistics Canada 1996: 366).

Some education administrators see highlighting Blackness as negative, as going against the consensual and dominant "colour blind" perspective of Canadian society. This perspective results in a lack of enthusiasm for research in the area of race and difference. The fact that the African Canadian population is numerically small (particularly in Edmonton) reinforces the view of the dominant research community and funding bodies that it is not statistically significant. Often, African Canadians as a social group are only considered worthy of research when they are per-ceived as a problem for the dominant White society. This view fails to recognize that, regardless of the number of African Canadians living in a community, our stories will provide insights into the formation of racial codes and meanings in the wider society. Further, the experiences of Blacks who are isolated in a predominantly White community will be different from, yet similar to, the experiences of African Canadians who have grown up in areas with a significant African Canadian presence. The meaning and consequences of being an African Canadian will differ according to vari-ables of geography, history, class, gender, sexual orientation, age, and the social norms of the period.

That multiple factors are associated with being an African Canadian adolescent corresponds with the valid critique of theorists who question whether the construct of "Black" is built upon the notion of there being a restrictive Black "essence" (Bhabha 1990; hooks 1992). How can research focus on one specific human dimension related to physiology when the group under investigation has a variety of lifestyles and perspectives? In adopting the term Black, I recognize that it is a social construct, as is White. By social construct, I mean that the label White is not based on biology, but is created and given meaning by social interactions and interpretations within society. While there are structural forms of oppression that Black people experience in common, across gender, class and geographic loca-tion, there has to be recognition that differences also exist in relation to gender, class, sexual orientation and geographic region. As Miles and Phizacklea argue, "[I]t is the unique experience of Blacks of racial exclusion that is the essence of Black ethnicity" (1977: 495). Failure to recognize the heterogeneity of Black identity and to choose instead to treat social groups as homogeneous and stable entities may be described as *essentialist* (Carby 1982; hooks 1984; Wallace 1990). Anti-essentialists call for a recognition that differences in the political and cultural behaviour of minority women and men are determined by social and historical contingencies and not by some essential checklist of innate biological or cultural characteristics (Wallace 1990). The advantage of being sensitive to and challenging essentialism in Black communities is that such a position provides the opportunity to undermine racism based on the notion of an "authentic Black" identity. Perhaps a useful way out of the anti-essentialist versus essentialist debate is to recognize that at times it is "strategic" for us to essentialize ourselves as a group in order to gain social changes (Spivak 1993: 3). This strategy is illustrated in Chapter Two where I discuss the ways in which the African Canadian community responds and adapts to the varying provincial expressions of racism.

Stuart Hall illustrates a way around essentializing when, in discussing Black Caribbean identity, he recommends that "we might think of Black Caribbean identity as formed by two axes or vectors, simultaneously operative: the vector of similarity and continuity; and the vector of difference and rupture" (1990: 226). Recognizing Black identity as not static or fixed allows me to avoid charges of undertaking an essentialist discussion of race and take a position that acknowledges "multiple black identities, varied black experiences" (hooks 1992).

If identity is recognized as a learned rather than a biological part of one's being, it is analytically more useful to think of a process of "identification" rather than identity. This approach enables one to recognize identification as an ongoing process (Hall 1992: 287). Black identity is not a single all-encompassing sense of self. Identification with a Black identity is influenced by how easy or difficult it is to be recognized as Canadian, for example, by the wider non-Black community. As Dei points out, we have to

> recognize and understand that identity is defined by who the individual is, how the individual self is understood in relation to others, and how such constructions of social identities match or do not match what people actually do in their lives. (1996: 59)

Focusing on forms of social interaction and the perceptions of a specific group of Black students enables me to partly answer the question of how the students' race and ethnicity relates to their schooling. Racialization of the lives of Black students emerges in their interpretations of and the meanings they give to their everyday life and school experiences. If we take seriously the remark that "if men [sic] define social situations as real, they are real in their consequences" (Thomas and Thomas 1928: 572), then we need to be able to gain access to those virgin interpretations. Linking the Thomases statement to race we can postulate that each actor's and, more importantly, each group's definition of a social situation and each group's racialized frame of reference—which shapes that definition—informs their social action and thereby their social reality (Figueroa 1991: 35). Although schools exist as institutions with overt aims and objectives, not every group within that school experiences these objectives in the same way (Anyon 1981; Ogbu 1992; Solomon 1992). This is the case for students as well as for teachers, as indicated by research on the hidden curriculum (Jackson 1968; LeCompte 1978).[4] Often investigations of this aspect of school life reveal the subtle ways that schools as institutions bring about certain outcomes as a result of the roles and identities that pupils adopt (Willis 1977). The meanings, attitudes, outlooks and predisposition that people bring to bear on the situations they encounter, as well as the situations themselves, have a history; that is, situations are the outcome of a "historical run of experience" (Blumer and Duster 1980; Mead 1934). Therefore, since racialization is present in mainstream society, most students have a historical run of racial experiences, even if that history does not include interaction with other racial and ethnic groups (Frankenberg 1993).

Placing Myself in the Research

It can be argued that most Canadians subscribe to a liberal philosophy, one that leads many educators (and other members of society) to believe that ignoring the race/ethnicity of students results in their being treated equally. Some educators come to believe that by adopting this colour-blind attitude they are ensuring that "race" does not affect the way in which students receive and perceive their schooling—a position akin to seeing "sameness in different color" (Chalmers 1997: 72). This approach is illustrated in an extract from my research journal of February 25, 1994.

> Met with Mr. Admin and Ms. Strator who are in the Student Services Department. Mr. Admin suggested that I explain myself. Seemed slightly antagonistic towards me. He said that the nature of my research was sensitive, especially in light of the beating that had taken place in one of the high schools that I wanted to visit. He stated that they did not keep records of students' ethnic origins.

In comparison to the United States, relations between racial groups in Canadian society are portrayed as being harmonious; "race" is seen as having little effect on the experiences of students. But is this true? Is this comparison and perspective supported by the experience of Black students?

Formulation of an area of inquiry often reflects one's raced, classed and gendered positions within society. With that in mind, I believe it is useful to indicate how and why I became interested in Black youths and their experiences of schooling. This positioning of myself recognizes that knowledge and meanings are produced from a specific social and political understanding of the world. We all have a standpoint from which we speak even if we do not recognize it as such. I should add that while explaining how I came to this area of research may reveal the filter through which I wrote this book, it does not provide a complete guide to the embedded bias that result from the various ways in which I have been constructed.

Perhaps the most important factor in my recent past has been my immigration to Canada. My emigration from England gave me the opportunity to reconstruct and compare how race operates in another White-dominated society. The conceptual development of my research question has been influenced by my social and cultural identity as a Black woman who has lived in White-dominated societies. For me this inquiry is a continuation of my ongoing interest in the issue of "race" and how its construction affects the social, economic and political lives of those not belonging to the dominant groups. Having been active in political and community groups working towards a social, political and economic transformation of society I have personally experienced as well as observed the interlocking oppressions of race, class and gender.

Although English and Canadian societies differ, and the umbilical cord of dominion status has been cut, philosophies and ideologies in each location continue to influence one another. Therefore, as both a newcomer to Canada and a Black woman—I wondered how a society with similar roots, values and structures to other more tension-ridden democracies could have achieved the harmonious multiculturalism the rhetoric suggests. Further, years of working as an educator in the school system means that I have a heightened awareness of both the nuances of racism and the difficulties of shifting the approach of the school from assimilation to anti-racist.[5]

In England, racism is more explicit and is recognized as a source of potential social and educational conflict open to political manipulation (Gilroy 1991; Hall 1993). In contrast, Canadian society is more reluctant than the U.K. to openly recognize conflict. The country is generally portrayed as a conflict-free multicultural society (Schick 1995). This construction of Canada as "gentle" in terms of its acceptance of those visibly different from the dominant group is, as argued above and in Chapter Two, partly related to Canadians' myopic sense of being better than those south of the border, and to an ignorance of Canada's racial history.

While being an outsider gave me a degree of insight into racialization in Canada, I still had to develop an understanding of the world of the students who were to be the focus of my inquiry. Although I am raced and gendered in ways common to the students, my experiences are different. A picture of the students' world was gained from interviewing individuals with different fields of interest, ranging from education to community work, and from attending outside school events in which the students were involved, including a court hearing.

Methodology, School and Students

Since race is a social construct that is ascribed to a group of people, I felt it was appropriate to use focus groups to gain insight into the youths' "natural" vocabulary when discussing the issues of racialization and identities. Focus groups provided an opportunity to view the times when youths agreed on issues, when they were willing to challenge each other and how they responded to such challenges (Morgan 1988: 18). All the focus groups developed their own dynamic as the participants recalled similar experiences and, in some cases, corroborated and elaborated on common experiences.

Many of the students welcomed the opportunity to share their experiences in the focus group. After one focus group, I was approached by a group of four girls who wanted to know why I had not invited them to be interviewed and become part of the project. One of them dramatically rolled up her sleeve and said, "Aren't I Black enough?" The incident illustrates the degree of interest shown by the students who volunteered for the research, as well as the contentions around who is seen as "Black enough." They wanted their voices to be heard! My journal extract demonstrates that for another student the focus groups were cathartic—perhaps they are a better way of self-expression than writing, which is often the *modus operandi* in classrooms:

> At the end of our session, one of the participants introduces me to another student who he suggests should get involved "'Cause we have some heavy deep discussion man." (Personal Journal, River High, April 8, 1994)

I selected the schools for this research on the basis of observation because, in line with the colour-blind attitude, no records of student origins were kept. Recognizing that identity is layered and crossed by gender (hooks 1981), I held three focus groups with a group of boys and another three with a group of girls in each of the two Edmonton schools, as well as individual interviews with students and thirteen teachers.

In terms of differences, River High is seen by many within the educational community as a school with a strong academic tradition. Its reputation is based mainly on the academic programs it offers and the fact that many of its students go on to university and other higher education institutions. Alternatively, Valley High offers fewer academic programs and is situated in an area that has a higher level of socio-economic problems. Though many of its students go on to university and other post-secondary institutions, its past reputation as a school with a vocational focus remains. A teacher who had worked at both schools compared them:

> Ms. Chalk: *In River High two-thirds of the students were serious students who had their life together and going forward. One-third were unmotivated and struggling . . . . In Valley High two-thirds were struggling, and one-third were as good as any student at River High . . . . At River High more Black students had a broader experience . . . [whereas in Valley High] welfare was more of a lifestyle . . . . [Basically] a school is academic because of the children who go there.*

Another teacher, who had also worked at both schools, reiterated the differences:

> Mr. Elastic: *River High doesn't have the vocational program that Valley High does . . . . We [at Valley High] have a real gamut of high academic achievers and then we have low academic achievers. River High was all the same. You couldn't take "shop" at River High.*

Despite the schools having differing intakes in terms of the students' socio-economic status, the students' identifications within these schools are complex and multiple and do not necessarily relate to simple conceptions of "class," "race" or gender.

The twenty-six females and twenty-three males interviewed for the research were in grades 10, 11 and 12. Their ages ranged from fifteen years to twenty years. Most of the students were born in Canada, but a significant majority had parents who were born in the Caribbean. A few of the students had immigrated to Canada during their junior high school years. While the students had a critique of schooling and society, this did not mean that they rejected the benefits of schooling or education, or that some students did not succeed (Codjoe 1997).

Research findings (Goetz and LeCompte 1984; Labov 1973) have indicated that the gender of the interviewer may well affect the social situation and verbal behaviour in a group. To counter this, Malcolm Azania, a then education student with a wide knowledge of popular culture, assisted me as a moderator for the male focus groups. Having Malcolm's assistance was useful, not just in terms of developing a rapport in the male focus groups, but also because I was able to discuss the male sessions with him and hear his interpretation of what had taken place.

In presenting the student narratives in this book, I try to create a binocular effect so that their voices stand clear and distinct in Chapters Three, Four and Five next to my interpretations in Chapters One, Two and Six. This "stereo vision involves two images: the image of the left eye (the ethnographer's) and the image of the right eye (the native's)" (Werner and Schoepfle 1987: 311). My aim is to apply this approach, or "binocular" metaphor (Kluckhohn 1949), to my consideration of individual experiences and their broader context to develop two differing images (mine and the research participants') that can be brought together to focus on the issue of learning to be Black in a White-dominated society. Without this binocular vision there is a danger of over-theorizing and thus devaluing the students' perspectives, a form of massaging the data in order to create a particular hypothesis. The research reflects students in specific schools at a particular historical moment. As adolescents they are experimenting with what it means to be Black. There is no guarantee that their views and perceptions will remain beyond their school years.

Finally, I want to caution that carrying out research is problematic at the best of times but when the issue under discussion is related to race and racialization certain pressures and responsibilities come to mind as I attempt to "get it right." In one focus group this was crystallized for me when a student indicated:

> *What you are doing right now is awesome because you are like speaking for all of us with this [research].* (Yvonne)

Although the theme of identity and how it articulates with racialization is highlighted in this book, this is not the one and only perspective that can be gained from reading the students' narratives. As with most human interaction, what was going on within the schooling experiences of these students was complex and it operated on many levels relating to class and gender as well as race. The lens I used for my interpretation was open to a wide range of possibilities. Many insights can be gained if we listen closely to what the students have to say.

PART II: UNDER THE GAZE

> Despite their small numbers, the history of blacks in Alberta's two
> main cities has been a microcosm of the larger North American
> urban black experience of the 20th century. The economic position
> of blacks, the role of the church within the black community, the
> patterns of race relations (including discrimination in housing and
> employment) and the roots of changing attitudes towards blacks
> have mirrored the larger black experience. (Palmer and Palmer
> 1981: 9)

Analysis of the social experiences of Blacks based solely on ethnic
dimensions cannot fully account for the variety of interactions they experience (Simon 1987). While ethnic categories based primarily on culture fit
with the concept of multiculturalism and the Canadian mosaic, they do not
capture the nuanced social constructions of race formulated within wider
society. Indeed, in the Statistics Canada (1996) data referred to earlier,
most groups are identified by region of origin. In addition African Canadians are categorized as Black rather than by geographic region, a desig-
nation that surely must read as official recognition of "Black" as a social
construction.

Unlike some areas of North America, Edmonton does not have a Black
neighbourhood. For the most part, the Black population is interspersed
within "mixed" areas. According to the 1996 Statistics Canada census,
Edmonton is the fourth most diverse city in Canada and 14 percent of the
total city's population could be deemed "visible minorities" (Mitchell
1998: A1).[6] Yet in spite of the absence of ghettoization, and in spite of the
legal support for pluralism, racism is still evident. In terms of school life,
Seifeddine's study *Changing Mosaic* (1994) reveals that African students
suffer name-calling and racial slurs more than other ethnic groups. Fifty-
seven percent of students of African descent indicated that someone in
school had acted towards them in a negative way because they looked
different. Academically, it is difficult to determine the success levels of
African Canadians in the Edmonton education system since records of
ethnic or "race" origins are not kept. Thakur has suggested,

> [A]lthough we have not found widespread "streaming" or "track-
> ing" in Alberta schools, the fact is that it does exist. And, as we
> have demonstrated, in some cases it is strongly resisted, particu-
> larly by the more well-to-do parents . . . . If the process of status
> displacement and downward mobility continues, streaming or

tracking will become widespread with generations. (1988: 23)

Organization of the curriculum has been based on the "accommodation" of Black students and the lived experiences of other marginalized groups rather than on "inclusion" within the main body of the curriculum. Further, a report by Multicultural Leaders, *Working Sub-Committee Report on Discrimination in Schools* (1993), also found the existence of racism in Edmonton schools. Similarly a report by the Edmonton Social Planning Council, *Because of Colour* (1992), found racial tension in some neighbourhoods and a low participation rate among minority groups in the management structures of community leagues.[7]

For many students, the very fact of being Black within a society constructed as White highlights their presence and reinforces a sense of "otherness." Some students see themselves as highly visible and often "under the gaze" of Whites in general and particularly figures of authority. Being "under the gaze" also makes these students see and experience themselves as "Other." This process of othering is used by figures of authority as a way of monitoring and questioning how these students use social spaces. Their ability to perceive themselves as Other and then to alter or not alter their behaviour is an important part of their coming to define themselves as Black. Blacks within a White society come to be seen by the dominant group and other groups as marked and not representative of the "norm," which is centred in Whiteness. Dyer provides a useful insight into the process of normalization: "black is always marked as a color, and is always particularizing; whereas white is not anything really, not an identity, not a particularizing quality, because it is everything—white is no color, because it is all colors" (1988: 20).

The bond between many of the Black students interviewed is their reaction to a White-dominated society that "marks their colour," as well as a sense of what bell hooks (1992) calls "collective memory," a shared knowledge of Black history and contemporary experiences. The significance of this shared memory is captured by Jonathan Arac's formulation:

> [T]he process of remembering can be a practice which: transforms history . . . from a judgement on the past in the name of a present truth to a "counter-memory'" that combats our current modes of truth and justice, helping us to understand and change the present by placing it in a new relation to the past. (1986: xviii)

The students' narratives indicate that the way in which others perceive them in society and the way in which they perceive themselves affects the construction of their various identities. Although aspects of culture related to their differing geographical origins (the Caribbean, continental Africa and North America) is important, so too is the identity they create from being "raced" (Hall 1992: 308).

Shopping malls are sites where many of the Black students feel "under the gaze." This situation is exacerbated by the close proximity of the high schools to the malls. The physical location increases the likelihood of the Black students coming into dispute with mall security staff over which areas of the malls they can occupy, and how they occupy those spaces.

As with school, the students perceive that the mall security guards often seek them out as a group to ask them to "move on" or to remove articles of clothing that signify perceived gang membership and therefore potential violence:

> Toni: *You're not allowed to wear bandannas in [Wonder Mall], because they say it symbolizes gangs.*

> Eldridge: *We used to hang in the malls, but you get too much trouble now.*

The treatment Toni describes is not unique to Black students; youths from other raced, ethnic or socio-economic groups may also be seen as potential troublemakers. However, with Black youths and other so-called visible minorities the process is one of racialization because the mall security respond to the physical appearance of the youths and to the assumptions associated with specific forms of clothing such as bandannas and jackets.

Both male and female students indicated that if they walked into a store, someone watched or followed them to make sure they were not stealing. These reactions of mall staff are certainly not specific to Edmonton. In studies done in Nova Scotia and Ontario Black youths allude to a perception of being watched closely in malls and shops (Black Learners Advisory Committee [BLAC] 1994; James 1990).

Males who "move" as a group and as individuals have also been put under the gaze by the police. Some youths recounted experiences of being stopped by the police at night, under the auspices of a being suspected of a crime:

> Malcolm: *One time I was pretty much pissed off, I had come from a party and got dropped off and then I hear this car screech to a halt. I felt a hand and this cop putting me into this car. They kept saying, "I know you're lying . . . ." Then they heard over the radio that they had caught the person. They didn't apologize; they just took off the cuffs and let me go.*

> Bobby: *One time I was walking with a Caucasian girl, and a cop*

pulled up . . . beside me and said "Are you okay, miss? Is this guy giving any trouble to you?"

For those youths who are developing a profile with the police, such as Eldridge, interaction with law enforcers was ongoing:

Eldridge: *Seems like the cops always want to blame everything on the Black youth . . . . The cops are always saying to me [that] I'm in [a gang] . . . . That's stupid 'cause those guys are always in jail for stupid things they do.*

The Controlling Gaze

The importance of the gaze is that it allows a dominant group to control the social spaces and social interaction of all groups. Blacks are made visible and invisible at the same time under the gaze. For example, when Black youth are seen it is often with a specific gaze that sees "the troublemaker," "the school skipper" or "the criminal." Thus they are seen and constrained by a gaze that is intended to control physical and social movement. The purpose of the gaze is that it should subdue those who receive it and make them wish to be invisible. The effect of receiving the gaze is indicated by Fanon when he states, "I slip into corners, I remain silent, I strive for anonymity, for invisibility. Look, I will accept the lot, as long as no one notices me!" (1967: 82).

Foucault describes control via the gaze as a process of "immersing people in a field of total visibility where the opinion, observation and discourse of others would restrain them from harmful acts" (1980: 153). What Foucault is describing is the way that social subjugation is achieved by social illumination. For these Black students, being under the gaze encourages them to police their own behaviour and censure themselves in certain locations where they interact with Whites. This self-censuring can be seen as an example of Blacks becoming compliant in their own social control since

there is no need for armed, physical violence, material constraints. Just a gaze. An inspecting gaze, a gaze which each individual under its weight will end by interiorising to the point that he is his own overseer, each individual thus exercising this surveillance over and against, himself. (Foucault 1980: 155)

Not all students who are put under the gaze respond by submitting and wishing to merge and become integrated into the social mainstream of school, denuded of their difference. As with all social interactions, there are choices to be made. However, gendered identity and socio-economic status, as well as being Black, filter these choices. For some of the youths discussed in this book, choosing not to submit to the gaze of control is seen as a form of resistance to White mainstream assimilation. Rather than submitting to the gaze, some Black students accentuate their visibility, thus providing a "glare" of light to interrupt the gaze. This "glare" can be achieved by a combination of dress, walk and attitude that is reinforced by moving in a group. For "glaring back" to be effective, both those sending the glare and those receiving it must have some form of non-verbal communication, otherwise the meaning of the interaction is lost. Stereotypes aid the communication and recognition between groups by offering constructs that have the potential for double meanings.

In River High the stereotype at work in the interaction between a group of White males and a group of Black males was that of the "uppity Black." Connotatively negative in White terminology but not necessarily accepted as so by Blacks, this term describes behaviour that has the potential to subvert the gaze. This process appeared to have taken place around a group of male students. As Eldridge stated:

> They look at you . . . the way you dress, and that stuff like that . . . . Black people dress different from White people . . . and the way we dress they always looks at us and say that we are in a gang . . . . It's like we walk around as friends but they take it the wrong way. We just move with the crowd.

A teacher verified this process of interpreting this group of young Black males the "wrong" way:

> Mr. Easel: We had a group of kids . . . and they would hang around together, almost an intimidatory [group] . . . . I don't know if they were trying to intimidate other people, but just the way they were posturing was an intimidating kind of thing.

The following group of young women shared their perspectives on how Eldridge's group of young males was perceived by some White students, males in particular.

> Lorraine: You should have seen Clerin. He used to carry himself with so much pride. The guy had so much self-respect. He'd wear anything, he was rough . . . he demanded respect.

> Pearl: It wasn't that he demanded it, it was there, you get it by the way you carry yourself . . . and they [Whites] didn't like it. They wanted you to bow down.

Lorraine: *The White people—they don't like it the other way round, for them to bow to you.*

Juliet: *The White boys especially didn't like it, I heard White boys in my class say, "That Clerin, [sarcastically] he thinks he's so fly, his body is all that."*

In reading Eldridge's narrative and that of Mr. Easel's, a teacher who recognizes the glare, and the three young women's interpretation of their fellow non-Black students' response to this glaring, it becomes evident that the Black youths' signification was achieved via posture, clothing and attitude.

I see this glaring as a form of resistance, but it can be interpreted in a variety of ways by non-Black society. In River High "Black style" could be seen as an innocent aspect of youth culture or as a more provocative tool of posturing and intimidation. Paula, a student, knew Eldridge's group and made the following observation about the "posturing" ascribed to a specific walk and gait when asked:

Jennifer: *Are young men anywhere noted for attitude?*

Paula: *Attitude is for girls, but for boys it's "acting tough," walking with a hip hop, "bouncing," "walking tough."*

This reference to the gait of young Black males as indicating a "new assurance" is echoed in Dick Hebdige's (1979) work on subcultures and Black youth in Britain.[8]

As Eldridge's group of young Black males came together in the school, the ability to posture and glare increased, as did the power of signification. In order for the gait and attitude of Eldridge's group to be recognized as signification, however, all youth have to understand the messages being conveyed. This understanding is gained from the video, magazine, film and TV images that all youths are exposed to even if they do not consciously relate to them. The students associated "dressing Black" with youths and youth lifestyle as depicted in popular films such as "Menace II Society" and "Boyz N' the Hood":

Lorraine: *They see "Menace II Society" and they think that we are all O-Dogs [a homicidal youth].*

Toni: *Or in the "hood" [neighbourhood].*

Everton, another student, further illustrated how these associations were

21

part of the everyday lives of teens:

> *Like I'm wearing a headband . . . and if I walk down the hallway,*
> *and if [I saw] one of those guys that didn't like it, they'd be like*
> *"You're from the hood now are you?"*

The result of this association of a specific style with violent characters is that often Black students who dress in a similar manner even if they are not violent, may be seen as posturing a toughness that makes them viable targets of aggression; this sequence illustrates the interconnectedness of style, stereotypes and signification.

Non-Black males' dislike of this posturing/glaring sometimes manifested itself in comments or verbal threats. The comments of a specific group of White males led them to physically challenge Eldridge's group of Black males. George described the reaction of fellow students to Eldridge's group of friends:

> George: *Intimidation is the biggest thing . . . . They [non-Blacks]*
> *figure that we are not the same as other Black guys in the school.*
> *I hear them talking about these other Black guys [Eldridge's*
> *group] . . . . A lot of people were saying, "Look at him wear his*
> *hat to the side . . . ." And a fight started out last year just because*
> *certain guys were dressing the way they were. Just the way they*
> *walk some guys think they are all that. They [non-Blacks] don't*
> *know that person for them to start judging them.*

Glaring is more than returning the gaze and perhaps even challenges "White invisibility," which, as hooks argues, is a way to deal with a Black gaze:

> In white supremacist society, white people can safely imagine that
> they are invisible to Black people since the power they have
> historically asserted, and even now collectively assert over Black
> people accorded them the right to control the Black gaze. To look
> directly was an assertion of subjectivity, equality. Safety resides
> in the pretence of invisibility. (1992: 168)

However, glaring also has its costs, and mainstream society can apply sanctions to those interrupting the controlling gaze. As Eldridge's group found out, applying this glaring strategy can result in other youths responding with aggression in order to smother their glaring and encourage them to submit to the gaze of the dominant group. Paradoxically, by resisting the dominance of the gaze of this specific group of White students, Eldridge and his friends were pushed into portraying a societal stereotype of violent Black males, a stereotype that itself on occasion resulted in White violence against them (a violence that the authorities excused as a reaction to "intimidation").

This discussion cuts through the notion that Canadian society is consistently pluralist and supportive of multiculturalism. It indicates instead that Canadian society is not open to difference but is seeking assimilation to a Eurocentric norm. A comment made by one student highlights this succinctly. In response to another student's comment that Canada was a salad bowl, Clara replied that if this was so then

the Whites are the green part; they dominate everything.

Concomitant with being "under the gaze" is a feeling of being very visible in social situations where Whites are in the majority. This visibility is a theme explored in sociological and psychological literature as well as by writers of African origins who examine interactions between Blacks and Whites. As a Black immigrant in France, Frantz Fanon succinctly explains this alienating experience: "I am being dissected under white eyes, the only real eyes. I am fixed. Having adjusted their microtomes, they objectively cut away slices of my reality. I am laid bare" (1967: 82).

Though expressed differently, the students described similar feelings about social situations in which they were in the minority:

Kathleen: *I go out with mainly Black . . . .*

Lilieth: *Cause you feel comfortable . . . they "know where you are coming from."*

Kathleen: *When you go to parties and stuff . . . when you walk in and you are the only Black person with a lot of White people, people tend to stare. Like you stand out. If you walk into a whole bunch of Black people you are integrated with everyone. You are not a big eyesore.*

Milton: *[When you are] with Whites you are always Black, they refer to your Blackness . . . with other Blacks you are just another person.*

That racial solidarity may result from a sense of discomfort, and experienced racial boundaries are highlighted clearly in Paula's comment:

I wouldn't go to a party with a White person, because they wouldn't like the same type of music, I might go to a movie but not a party. I might go with an African. I think that if I went with a Black person that I didn't know I might have more fun than with a White person that I knew.

The response of some students to White dominance was to create their own identity. This identity affected the level and degree of socializing that some students engaged in after school. Although expressed in ways that can be seen as essentialist, these students nonetheless were sophisticated in their attempts to form a group based on being Black, as well as on their culture and ethnicity. As will be seen, this strategic use of essentialism was not based on any biological essence but on lived experiences of the historical and social constructions present in society.

Grades 1–8, Toles School, Amber Valley, Alberta. c. 1942

NOTES

1. All the names used in this text have been changed in order to maintain the project participants' anonymity, with the exception of Malcolm Azania, my co-moderator for the male focus groups, and Jennifer Kelly, the author.

2. All these theorists challenge the conception of identity as fixed and centred. Hall's (1992) work in Britain has shifted to a more open conception of Black identity that is intersected by class and gender. Gilroy's (1993) analysis spans the U.S. and Britain and makes links between cultural formations in these countries, which undermine an ethnic absolutist position adopted in the U.S. hooks' (1992) work in the U.S. and Himani Bannerji's (1995) work in Canada reveals the interlocking ways in which race, class and gender relate to identity.

3. The McGill Consortium (Torczyner 1997) assists ethnic communities to conduct research that relates to their demography. In the 1997 findings, the consortium identifies two official counts that can be gleaned from 1991 Census Canada information. The first is a restrictive identification that is based on a single component of identity and looks solely at responses to an ethnic origin/ancestry question. This count estimates that the population with "Black origins" is 224,620. The second count is comprised of the population included in the first identification plus a population that is deemed likely to be Black, even though it has not explicitly reported this. The population derived from this latter count is 504,290.

4. The hidden curriculum is a sociological concept coined by Philip Jackson in his 1968 book, *Life in Classrooms*. Jackson uses the term to describe the unofficial three Rs of rules, routines and regulations that must be learned by pupils in order to survive comfortably in most classrooms.

5. Anti-racism education may be defined as an action-oriented strategy for institutional, systemic change to address racism and the interlocking systems of social oppression (Dei 1996: 25). George Dei's book, *Anti-Racism Education: Theory and Practice* (1996), offers an excellent explanation of the aims and purposes of anti-racism education in a Canadian context.

6. According to the Employment Equity Act (1986) "visible minorities are persons (other than Aboriginal persons), who are non-Caucasian in race or non-white in colour" (Statistics Canada 1996: 97). The term visible minority is contentious because it posits Whites as the "norm" against which others are visible.

7. Community leagues organize activities and programs—sports and social— within designated areas of the city. Funded partially by the city council, they also fundraise and are governed by the society's Act (Alberta Society's Act, May, 1996).

8. Hebdidge, in *Subculture: the Meaning of Style* suggests that as part of the process of offering a challenge to the dominant narrow definitions of themselves, many of the youths in his research adopted a style whereby "the very way they moved implied a new assurance—there was more deliberate 'sass,' 'more spring, less shuffle'" (1979: 41).

Chapter Two

Racialization:
The Social Construction of Race

Maya: *They [non-Blacks] always say "Why should you guys be mad at us for what our ancestors did?"*
Grace: *They are [being racist] now only it's not as noticeable and you can't see it as easily.*
Zora: *When they say that, [I say], "But we're still paying for the image that our ancestors have, we are still paying for that slavery image . . . . We are still linked to that history, but yet they want to totally forget about theirs.*

This chapter outlines the historical construction of race in Canadian society, including the racialization of Canadian identity. This provides a framework against which to read the student narratives. The concept of Black identity is discussed using recent theories in cultural studies. In discussing the concept of racialization, that is, how physical differences come to assume certain meanings and expectations for human behaviour and interaction, I look at:

- how race, as a concept, is constructed and used as a basis for differentiation and social marginalization;
- the way in which the meaning of race is interpreted historically and presently;
- how the definition of race is used to construct meanings that maintain the social and economic dominance of a particular group within society.

In recent years, the meanings associated with "race" have reflected developments in post-structuralist, feminist and post-modern theory. Increasing sensitivity to and recognition of difference and diversity in many societies have influenced understandings of race. Looking at contemporary Canadian society, I examine how the meanings of race and identity have become linked and the ways in which a raced identity becomes problematic within a society that does not recognize the category or existence of race. This examination provides insights into the racialization process and how collective identities become constructed as a result of that process.

The discussion in this chapter reflects the fragmented and complex nature of the collective identity of being Black. It attempts to maintain an eclectic theoretical base which can deal with the recognized complexity of "race" and "difference," and yet still remain linked to issues of dominance and subjugation. Although not the focus of this chapter, it should be noted that racialization as a process was critiqued by some Whites, whether the issue was segregated schooling, restricted immigration strategies or enlistment practices during the 1914–18 war.

The chapter provides a background for the following questions: How do the Black students I met with come to perceive and react to society in the ways that they do? As noted earlier what is it within Canadian society that made Clara, a student, suggest that,

> *if Canadian society is supposed to be a salad bowl then the Whites are the green part; they dominate everything!*

So What's Race Got to Do with It?

As indicated in Chapter One, terminology is problematic when discussing the concept of race. Does it exist? Is it an ideological construct? If it is an ideological construct, does it not have concrete material effects on peoples' lives? The definition of "race" has undergone various changes in the recent past. Currently race is recognized by some as a social relationship (Banton 1977). David Smith argues that it is essential to maintain the concept of race because, "unlike ethnic identity, racial identity and/or difference is immutable, manifest and normally unambiguous in multiracial societies and contexts" (cited in Mason 1986: 6). According to Smith, physical differences are markers of status whether or not other cultural differences are present. Because they have a genetic foundation, they are both permanent and hereditarily transmitted, and thus inferior or superior statuses are transmitted from one generation to another. Other scholars, while recognizing the powerful impact of the social definitions of observable physical differences, recommend either that the term "race" be set aside (Montague 1974) or that it be used to refer, not to a subspecies but, as van den Berghe puts it, to "a socially defined group which sees itself and is seen by others as being phenotypically different from other groups" (1983: 222).

Race as an Objective Condition
Many of the liberal and radical theories around race, although "committed to a social rather than biological interpretation of race, nevertheless slip into a kind of objectivism about racial identity and racial meaning" (Omi and Winant 1993: 6). Abstractly acknowledged to be a socio-historical construct, race in practice is often treated as an objective fact; one simply

is one's race. Objectivist treatments that lack a critique of the constructed character of racial meanings also cannot account for the wide-ranging experiences of race. Therefore if one does not act "Black" or "White," it is seen as deviance from the norm. Critiques of this perspective suggest that it cannot grasp the process-oriented and relational character of racial identity and racial meaning; it denies the historical and social comprehensiveness of the race concept; it cannot account for the way actors, both individual and collective, have to manage incoherent and conflictual racial meanings and identities in their everyday lives (Omi and Winant 1993). In other words, this perspective does not recognize the concept of racial formation.

The ideological construct of race can be understood as a tightly knit set of beliefs organized around a few central values. Ideology is thought to work by imposing usually liberal, metaphysical abstractions, which conceal and obscure the real exploitative relations (Billig 1982). Thus we can understand the function of ideology as one of obscuring the exploitative relations.

Robert Miles (1988) recognizes race as an ideological construct but cautions that as such it should have no real analytic status in the work of the sociology of race relations. He further reveals that the process of attributing meaning results in the reification of real social relations into ideological categories and leads to a commonsense acceptance that race is an objective determinant. As such Miles adopts a perspective that substitutes the term "racialization" for race, a move that emphasizes the social construct dimension of race. He views "racialization" or "racial categorization" as a process whereby meanings are attributed to certain patterns of physical variation.

> Within this process of racialization, the ideology of racism plays a central role by offering criteria upon which signification can occur, attributing negative correlates to all those possessing the real or alleged criteria, and legitimating consequent discriminatory behaviour or consequences. (Miles 1988: 9)

It is this understanding of racialization that is used within this book, with the recognition that racialization has concrete impacts. In other words, I examine how "through the process of racializing society, social groups are distinguished and subjected to differential and unequal treatment on the basis of supposedly biological, phenotypical and cultural characteristics" (Dei 1996: 25).

The concept of race is further complicated by it being used as both an ideological concept and a tool of analysis within society. In some ways one needs to deny the validity of biological race while affirming the social significance and effect of these categories—race is nuanced with contradictions. One way out of this theoretical impasse is to view race as a process in which certain groups are "raced" and then awarded power, status and prestige on the basis of that "racing"; others are denied these things on the basis of how they have been raced.

Even though race has little to do with biology, it continues to have social significance. Omi and Winant (1993), who analyze race in terms of racial formation, suggest that theorists who treat race as either purely ideological or objective fail to recognize the salience a social construct can gain over half a millennium or more of diffusion, or enforcement, as a fundamental principle of social organization and identity formation. They maintain that in everyday life race is an almost indissoluble part of our identities. "Our society is so thoroughly racialized that to be without racial identity is to be in danger of having no identity" (Omi and Winant 1993: 5).

Early Days: Race as Hereditary

Race as a form of classification developed hand-in-hand with the scientific exploration of human origins (Banton 1967, 1977). Whites incorporated its usage into racist theory as it purported to offer an explanation of and justification for the exploitation and subordination of Blacks. Racist theory was built on an ideology that upheld the notion of polygenesis, or the creation of human beings from multiple sources, as formulated by David Hume in late eighteenth century Europe:

> I am apt to suspect the Negroes, and in general all the other species of men (for there are four or five different kinds) to be naturally inferior to the whites. There never was a civilized nation of any other complexion than white, nor even any individual eminent in action or speculation. No ingenious manufactures amongst them, no arts, no sciences . . . . Such a uniform and constant difference could not happen, in so many countries and ages, if nature had not made an original distinction betwixt these breeds of men. (cited in Pieterse 1992: 41)

Hume's commentary, although racist and factually incorrect, provides an insight into the nineteenth-century ideology of race—thinking that has influenced many of the understandings of race that circulate in present day. Within such statements is an understanding of "races" as distinct categories contained within a biologically determined hierarchy. This biological determination was given further credibility in the mid-nineteenth century by Comte de Gobineau's four-volume publication *Essai sur l'inégalité des races humaines*. In his volumes Gobineau praises the Germanic race as the

29

aristocratic race and reveals that "purity was the hallmark and the necessary condition of civilization: a mixture of races was the cause of decadence, of the decline of civilization, for in every mixture the power race would predominate" (Pieterse 1992: 49). Biological determinism was the ideology that was common in Canadian society during the eighteenth, nineteenth and early twentieth century. This was the filter that was used to racialize the experiences of Blacks who came to Canada.

Canadians of African descent have a recorded presence on Canadian soil since 1605 when Mattieu da Costa was acknowledged as an interpreter working with Champlain. Over the next century most Blacks who arrived were accompanying their masters and mistresses as slaves, or were fleeing persecution in the United States. Settlement patterns and the reception they received varied according to the prevailing economic conditions and the specific province to which they immigrated.

The first Blacks in the colonies gained their freedom as the colonies abolished slavery early in the nineteenth century. A large community of free Black United Empire Loyalist settled in Nova Scotia after the American Revolution (1776–83), taking up land grants as they did so. Black slaves from the War of 1812, having sought refuge behind the British lines, supplemented this group in Nova Scotia "where they became the perpetual paupers known locally as the 'Refugees'" (Winks 1969: 165). The refugees were given barren land at Preston and Hammonds Plains, but since the land provided little future many moved to towns, especially Halifax, in search of work. Economically "the refugee Negroes had arrived at the worst of times. Cheap white labour was plentiful: sixteen thousand immigrants had come during the dozen previous years" (Winks 1971: 124). As a result of their inability to find work, many of these Black refugees remained in the lower socio-economic rungs of Nova Scotian society—their unemployment and socio-economic reality reinforcing existing stereotypes in White society that Blacks could not be self-sufficient.

Starting in the 1840s an area of Halifax became known as Africville and provided a separate community and escape for Blacks trying to avoid the discrimination they experienced in the White community. Africville came to symbolize the presence of African Canadians and the ways in which environmental and health issues coalesce with issues of racialization. For many years the city council of Halifax refused to pipe water and other basic public amenities into Africville. As a result the community became socially isolated and politically neglected. The council found the location to be an ideal site for various factories that were environmentally unacceptable to other areas of the city. In many ways their planning decisions exemplify what would be described as *environmental racism*. After much neglect, the Halifax city council decided to raze the community to the ground. Consistent with its historical relationship with the occupants of

Africville, the City showed very little respect for the wishes of those living in the community. A long-time resident analyzed the way in which the relationship between the council and the community was racialized:

> If they had been white people down there, the city would have been in there assisting them to build new homes, putting in water and sewers and building the place up . . . . There were places around Halifax worse than Africville was and the city didn't do to them what they did to Africville. (Boyko 1995: 171)

In Ontario, Blacks arrived in increasing numbers during the nineteenth century. Not only were slaves fleeing the U.S. via the Underground Railway, but "free" Blacks also came to Canada to escape the discrimination in the U.S. As Adrienne Shadd reveals, "Blacks were one of the largest groups to enter the country during the nineteenth century, when 40–60,000 fugitive slaves and free people 'of colour' sought refuge in Canada West (Ontario) between 1815–1860" (1991: 3). Thus the Black community consisted of differing groups who were fragmented by socio-economic status, periods of residency and often levels of education. Generally Blacks settled in isolated communities, in both Nova Scotia and Canada West: "[T]he Blacks were settled in the least desirable locations, usually on poor land or on farms of inadequate size, remote from the major centres of economic growth" (Walker 1980: 129).

Individual Blacks fought against the prejudice they encountered and some were able to succeed in economic terms and gain a degree of acceptability. But for Blacks collectively, their experiences of immigration were experiences of prejudice and exclusion. One example of "making it" within White mainstream society was the case of W.P. Hubbard who became a successful businessperson in Toronto and in 1894 was elected alderperson. He was elected thirteen times and often served as acting mayor. Ironically, even while he rose to acting mayor, his fellow African Canadians were barred from restaurants and other public facilities in Toronto.

Another example of how racial constructions vary is illustrated by the experience of Blacks who were fleeing from prejudice in California. This group was invited to settle on Vancouver Island in 1858, and also founded a self-contained farming community on Saltspring Island. In Vancouver a Black settler, Mifflen Gibbs, became a leader in the community and was a delegate to the 1868 Yale Convention that negotiated the terms for B.C. to join Confederation. The Black settlers were seen as an important bulwark against U.S. designs on British Columbia. One other reason for the initial acceptance of these pioneers may well have been that they were welcomed by the then Governor James Douglas, who, although passing as White, had a mother who was "either a West Indian mulatto or a Creole" (Winks 1971: 275). Further, these Black pioneers were skilled craftspersons and some were relatively wealthy.[1] Their success, however, did not prevent prejudicial acts that resulted in segregated churches, saloons and theatres dating from the 1860s until the mid-1870s (Conrad et al. 1993; Killan 1978; Winks 1971).

During the nineteenth century most African Canadians were located in Canada West (Ontario) and Nova Scotia. It was here that most opportunities existed for social mixing between Blacks and Whites. During this period education became an important tool for social mobility for all social groups in Canada. With the growth of common (public) schools during the 1840s, school promoters saw education as a tool of social formation whereby new citizens could be prepared for the emergent industrial society. For Blacks and other marginalized groups, education became racialized and, unlike other oppressive practices of the Canadian state, this racialization was overt.

Education

While some Whites were prepared to send their children to school with Blacks, many expressed distress at the thought of social mixing, which would lead to racial mixing:

> Of all the manifestations of Negrophobia the attempt to deny Negroes the equal use of public schools was the most successful. In communities where problems of land sales, voting rights or jury service never arose, a large number of white inhabitants agreed with efforts to keep Negro children from the schools. (Alexander Murray cited in Cooper 1991: 37)

Racial constructions and meanings in the wider society filtered Black educational experiences. The dominant conception of race as fixed and inherited reflected nineteenth-century British values and Darwinist beliefs in survival of the fittest that were reproduced to support the maintenance and dominance of the British Empire and the subjugation of Blacks in the U.S.

Schooling and race were issues that concerned those living in the growing towns of Canada West in the early nineteenth century. Despite the rationale that common schools were created to give all students a common experience, there were parameters to this common experience. Race and religion were seen as bases for segregation. Thus when the 1850 Common School Act was passed it contained section XIX that stated:

[I]t should be the duty of the Municipal Council of any Township, and of the Board of School Trustees of any City, Town or Incorporated Village, on the application, in writing, of 12 or more, resident heads of families, to authorize the establishment of one, or more, Separate Schools for Protestants, Roman Catholics, or coloured people. (cited in Walker 1980: 110)

Some historians suggest that Egerton Ryerson and the provincial government intended the section to be interpreted to mean that if twelve or more Black families wanted a separate school, they could elect their own trustees, use their own taxes and apply for an equivalent provincial grant to establish such a school. However the section also did not specify that this free education had to be provided in an integrated setting. This led to increased segregation of Black and White students. In reality, separate schooling had existed well before 1850. As early as 1830, Blacks had to set up their own schools because of prejudice. The 1850 Act served to intensify the exclusion of Black students, with many being obliged to attend "Negro Separate Schools." Since funding for these separate schools was dependent on the local community raising a portion of the necessary funds, the Black community always found itself at a disadvantage. Generally its community members were not as wealthy as those in the White Anglo mainstream.[2]

Animosity towards integrated schooling was rife among Whites. In London (Ontario) Whites insisted that Blacks be taught in separate schools because of the "inbred feeling of repugnance in the breast of almost every white person at hybridism, which must to some extent be the result of co-mingling" (cited in Conrad et al. 1993: 502). White-owned newspapers played a role in perpetuating the racial animosity. As *The Toronto Leader* stated in 1862 upon hearing that school authorities in London had voted to allow segregated schools when financially possible, "[W]here is the white man or woman in this city who would wish to see his daughter married to a black man" (cited in Winks 1971: 372).

Although these segregated schools gradually closed over the latter half of the nineteenth and early part of the twentieth century following court challenges, the discriminatory laws remained on the statute books of Ontario until 1964. In Nova Scotia, the reference to "different races" was dropped from the Education Act of the province in 1954, but actual desegregation did not occur until the following decade (BLAC 1994: 25). However geographic segregation has continued to reinforce social segregation in Nova Scotia and has led to present-day educational inequality. According to the BLAC (1994: 36) report:

The drop out rate indicates that the gap in educational attainment between the Black and the average Nova Scotian is growing, not declining. For persons over the age of 60, the level of educational disparity between Black Nova Scotians and the average Nova Scotian is 29 percent. But for younger people, the gap is 44 percent. While drop out rates may be declining, the education system is failing Black Nova Scotians, who are not experiencing the same improvements as the average Nova Scotian.

Black Resistance

Blacks were not passive recipients of racism. They fought the marginalization and raced constructions perpetrated by mainstream White society. Those Blacks critical of segregated schooling during the mid-nineteenth century often used their newspapers, the *Provincial Freeman* and the *Voice of the Fugitive*, to highlight the educational conditions for Black students. As Mary Ann Shadd, the editor, stated, "[T]he large and handsome school houses are erected for the children of Whites, but a single miserable contracted wooden building is set aside for the coloured taxpayers of the entire town" (cited in Cooper 1991: 77).[3]

As is the case today, the Black community's response to discrimination and racialized treatment was not homogenous, but was affected by variables such as whether they had entered Canada as "free" people or "slaves," as well as by their socio-economic background. In Canada West, for example, some believed the path to equality with the White society lay in setting up separate communities that were self-sufficient and free of charity. For these *communalists*, separate communities were a temporary strategy "where, with sympathy, patience and financial support, blacks could prepare themselves so that when they did enter white society they could do so with complete equality" (Walker 1980: 142). For others, the path to salvation lay with a more *integrationist* stance. For this group

> the geographical concentration of the blacks in organized communities would increase white prejudice for it would imply that blacks belonged apart and besides it would deprive the average white citizen of daily contact with blacks. The fugitives' continued dependence on charity would only offer justification to the racist view that blacks were unable to care for themselves and, therefore, belonged in slavery. (Walker 1980: 142)

These same racialized arguments emerged in debates about segregated schooling during the nineteenth and twentieth centuries. The question was whether Blacks should organize their own schools, which in many ways would provide a safer, less racist environment, or whether they should strive for the same education as Whites within the mainstream. As a compromise between the position of the communalist and integrationists, and in reaction to experiences with White society, Blacks set up "True Band Societies." The purpose of these societies is indicated clearly by Walker's description of the operation of the first such society formed at Amherstberg, Ontario, in 1854:

> When blacks had an argument among themselves they were en-
> couraged to bring them before the Band for settlement rather than
> airing them in public and thus contributing to an image of a
> squabbling disunited black community. Blacks were further en-
> couraged to disperse throughout the province, to prevent discrimi-
> nation by reducing black concentration in any one area. (1980:
> 118)

The aim of this True Band Society—to challenge some aspects of racialization—reflects the negative attitudes of a White society that viewed a concentration of Blacks as negative and threatening.[4]

Fitting the African into the Canadian

Using the concept of racialization to analyze Canadian society historically reveals a society in which cultural and national identities have been raced and constructed around a White norm. This dominance of a White norm is legitimated through the construction of various symbols and myths sur-rounding the creation and development of the Canadian state. While this book discusses the construction of Whiteness primarily in relation to African Canadians, this process of marginalization linked to racialization was also experienced by Chinese and First Nations people, East Indians, Southern and Eastern Europeans and others at the turn of the twentieth century. Although these groups were constructed at different periods as racially unacceptable for the Canadian state, the process of racialization was affected by and dependent upon their positioning in the Canadian racial hierarchy. This hierarchy was created in relation to White British values and attitudes. The following commentary on Ukrainian immigrants illus-trates that "Whiteness" is socially constructed and that its definition changes over time:

> It is quite possible that English-generations yet unborn will come
> to look up on the descendants of Galacian emigrants as their equals
> and friends; at the present time we do not so consider them. In view
> of their education, ideas, moral standards and mode of life, we
> justly regard them as inferiors. We are prepared to treat them with
> fairness and civility; we are not prepared to be bossed by them .
> . . . When it comes to investing a Russian yokel with authority to

dictate, in the Government's name, to English-speaking British subjects, we think that this is going too far, and anticipating too boldly on the future. We resent it as a humiliation; and it is unlikely that white men in this province will stand for it. ("H.D" a regular columnist for the *Vergreville Observer,* July 29, 1908; cited in Kostash 1977: 39)

This group was categorized as "non-White" and described by newspapers and religious leaders as drunks, kleptomaniacs and definitely not part of the "White race" in the early twentieth century. The terminology set them apart and excluded them from the economic and power structures of society (Kostash 1977). The commentary above illustrates clearly that racialization is based on more than skin colour and changes over time as certain groups are assimilated into mainstream "White" society. It is also worth noting that for groups whose origins were not in Europe and not phenotypically "White," this process of assimilation and acceptance has not been offered as readily.

While groups from Poland and Ukraine received a chilly welcome to the Canadian Prairies at the turn of the century, over time these groups have become assimilated into Canadian society. And, although this assimilation has not led to a consistent state of pluralism whereby these various ethnic groups share economic and political power, such groups have become recognized as part of the Canadian mosaic (Porter 1965). The ability to "pass" into the White group in Canadian society by changing one's name and learning to speak English constructs differences in the meanings attached to the immigrant experience. In contrast to the "meltable groups," the past experiences of those of Chinese, First Nations and African descent, for example, have resulted in economic, political and to some extent social marginalization. For African Canadians this marginalization has its roots in the racialization of their historical experiences. Though racialization is based on more that just skin colour, the saliency of this characteristic is undeniable. The physical differences between African Canadians and the dominant White society results in those physical aspects assuming certain meanings and being associated with particular types of human behaviour and interaction.

That Canadian society was constructed as White was not accidental. From 1900 to 1962 the desire to maintain a White European majority was realized through controlling immigration to ensure that preference was given to Anglo-Celtic stock (Palmer 1975). In other words, immigration was used to construct Canada as a White society, dominated primarily by those of European origins and built upon the values and lived experiences of that group. In terms of inclusion within the Canadian state, those of African descent, in spite of contributions to community development, were always regarded as not fully belonging and certainly were deemed unsuitable. The exclusion of Blacks from most recorded Canadian history results in an incomplete record that overlooks the real complexities of *historical multiculturalism* and negates instances where different ethnic and racial groups may well have come together to form alliances, as well as the times when they came into conflict.

National identities are not things with which we are born; we learn to claim them. Therefore a nation can be viewed as more than a political entity; it also produces meanings—a system of cultural representation (Hall 1992: 292). It is these systems of meanings that account for the power of nations to generate a sense of identity and allegiance. For example, our conception of Canadian identity and the meanings we attach to such an identity affect our views on whether the RCMP should be allowed to wear turbans or not. For those who equate a Canadian identity primarily with Anglo-Celtic derived values and culture, the wearing of a turban challenges this symbolic representation of what it means to be Canadian. In order to analyze the symbols and meanings attached to a Canadian identity it is useful to see what role African Canadians played in the production of what it means to be a Canadian.

The way in which maps of meanings are constructed often relates to the way that groups are included or excluded from a nation's history. Control over representation of the past can be used to achieve compliance with the aims and interests of those who exert power in the name of the state. Maria Alonso's concept of *idealization* is evident in the representation of Canadian national history whereby the past is *sanitized* and packaged in a way appropriate to national ideology (1988: 41). For African Canadians this idealization is reflected in the ways in which certain symbols such as the Underground Railway, protection of the Lion's paw and the guiding North Star came to indicate that the Canadian state was a haven for African Canadians fleeing the U.S.

The sanitization can be seen in the omission of accounts that recall the racist turn-of-the-century immigration policies or the segregated schooling of mid-nineteenth-century Ontario and twentieth-century Nova Scotia. The Canadian Civil Liberties Association revealed direct evidence of this sanitization of history when it reported in 1995 that the majority of graduating high school students in Metropolitan Toronto had little knowledge about Canada's history regarding civil rights abuses. Most students were unaware of past discriminatory practices such as the rejection of immigration applications on the basis of race, the legalized slavery of Blacks and Aboriginals and the internment of Japanese people during the Second World War (Grange 1995).

Immigration Practices

During the late nineteenth and early twentieth centuries the term "pioneer" became constructed as not only hardworking but also predominantly White, ignoring African Canadians and other raced groups who immigrated to the Canadian west during this period. Analysis of the immigrant experiences of Black settlers in early twentieth-century Alberta serves as a good example of how racialization was similar and yet differed on the basis of region, province and density of population. Over the period of 1905 to 1912 various strategies were employed by immigration authorities to discourage Blacks from moving to the Canadian west. Alberta was foremost among the provinces fighting to stem the flow of Black immigrants. Official organizations in Edmonton such as the Board of Trade and the Imperial Order Daughters of the Empire gathered petitions of protest to send to Ottawa.[5]

Analysis of the newspapers and political meetings during this period of immigration reveal differing and competing racial ideologies that often intersected with regional and political allegiances. For example, addressing a "representative gathering" at the Conservative Party club rooms in Edmonton, the following statement by Mr. Simmonds of Leduc highlights how some White inhabitants encoded "race" within existing regional animosities. Simmonds believed that immigration should reflect personal rights and individuals should be able to choose who they live with. Under no circumstances did he want his province to become "Black Alberta" as a result of a Black invasion, and he blamed the eastern-based Liberal government for being out of touch with Western sentiments:

> I can only see one way out of this difficulty . . . and this is to put the present government out of power and bring in one who will listen to our pleas . . . . Way down in Ottawa they do not think of the matter as seriously as we do, and therefore the interest is lacking. (cited in Shepard 1976: 107)

The Imperial Order Daughters of the Empire's appeal against Black immigration was gendered as well as raced. They used the stereotype of Black males as highly sexualized and animalistic to suggest that White women would not be safe if Black men lived in close proximity. In this case race, gender and class interlock illustrating the complexities of oppression whereby White middle-class women act in alliance with middle- and upper-class White males (who also oppress them).

The provincial newspapers at the height of the anti-Black immigration campaign published various stories that perpetuated and reinforced stereotypes of Black males as threatening. In April 1911 when a young girl was allegedly attacked at home and robbed by a Black man, the story became a rallying call for those who opposed Black immigration. The comments made by the reporter John Howey in Edmonton's *Bulletin*[6] describe the way in which many other news reporters embellished the story and reinforced hostility against Black immigration:

> Bad news travels fast, but like a snowball on the down grade the further it goes the bigger it grows. This particular item picked up a second negro and a flogging between Edmonton and Regina. It can hardly have been less than a murder and a lynching when it reached Toronto, and a free-for-all race war by the time it got to New York. (Shepard 1976: 105)

That the girl subsequently withdrew her allegations and admitted that there had been no robbery was, of course, not as widely disseminated by the various newspapers.

As part of seeing Blacks as a different species, immigration authorities excluded them on the spurious basis that they would not be able to stand the cold climate in Canada. The plausibility of this rationale depends on one's acceptance of the race theory that Blacks are biologically inferior and less adaptable to their environment.

What is noticeable about the way in which Canadian immigration authorities and citizens argued against the immigration of those of African descent is that these White Canadian citizens claimed that they were acting in the best interests of Blacks. Thus when a campaign was mounted at the turn of the twentieth century to prevent the immigration of "negroes" from Oklahoma, it was claimed that their arrival would result in discrimination against them! Such a formulation locates the origins of what is defined as problematic in the very presence of the migrant group. This interpretation reverses the sequence of events and obscures the active agent in the process—the host community.

Although provincial responses to immigration varied, this was more by degree than scale since most provinces were against Black immigration whether from the United States or from the Caribbean. Thus in 1911, while the western boards of trade were petitioning the federal government to stop American Blacks from taking up Canadian farms in Alberta and Saskatchewan, the *Montreal Herald* reported in a rather militaristic tone that the fifty-eight "dark-skinned" domestics from the Caribbean were the advance guard for others to follow. Again, the fear of large numbers of Blacks was evident.

Analysis of immigration to eastern provinces and the Maritimes during the early twentieth century reveals a picture in which Blacks provided a reserve army of labour, employed in a "split labour market" where they were paid less than White workers for doing the same work (Calliste 1993/

94). For example, migrant workers from the Caribbean were allowed into Nova Scotia but were channelled into menial jobs at local foundaries on the stereotypical assumption that they were accustomed to a hot climate. What this reinforced was a representation of Blacks as mentally, physically and socially inferior and incapable of doing work requiring intellect. As with Blacks emigrating from the U.S. to Alberta and Saskatchewan, health and financial requirements for immigration were applied stringently towards Caribbean Blacks. When the latter procedure failed, officers were privately encouraged to exclude Caribbean Blacks on the basis that they were likely to become "public charges."

Immigration officials and the government maintained a "Whiteness" to Canadian identity while stating openly that there was no official ban on Blacks. Blacks were perceived as sources of temporary labour to be exploited as necessary, not as long-term Canadian citizens. The general sentiment among Maritime immigration officials was that

> [t]here are certain countries from which immigration is encouraged and certain races of people as suited this [country] and its conditions, but Africans no matter where they are from are not among the races sought, and, hence, Africans no matter from what country they come are in common with the uninvited races,[7] not admitted to Canada. (cited in Calliste 1993/94: 135–36)

Constructions of the worth of peoples of African descent as immigrants continued until as late as 1955 when immigration officials used arguments reminiscent of early 1900s:

> It is the experience, generally speaking, that coloured people in the present state of the white man's thinking are not a tangible asset, and as a result are more or less ostracized. They do not assimilate readily and pretty much vegetate to a low standard of living . . . many cannot adapt themselves to our climatic conditions. (cited in Calliste 1993/94: 133)

What is particularly noticeable about this comment is that while the descriptor of "coloured" has replaced that of the "Negro," the same negative stereotypes persist.

Canadian society's construction of racism has been affected by its proximity to its rival, the U.S. If the U.S. is used as a gauge of racism, Canadian society will always appear more racially innocent—comparison with the U.S. provides a hiding place for racism in Canadian society. Issues of racism that have reached the surface of Canadian society have often been blamed on un-Canadian attitudes in an effort to distance Canadian society from any complicity in racism. In Alberta in the 1950s instances of discrimination "without exception were blamed on the several thousand Americans living in the Province" (Winks 1971: 473). Interestingly, Canada's relationship to the U.S. proved advantageous to African Americans coming to Alberta in 1911. Because of the newly signed "reciprocity agreement"[8] the Canadian government was unwilling to reject outright American citizens, even if they were Black (Shepard 1976: 115).

Although without a doubt much of the racism against Blacks could be attributed to American sources, there were other origins as well. European countries from which many non-Black immigrants came were filled with the negative images, stereotypes and representations of Africans used to justify colonialism. Jan Pieterse (1992), in *White on Black,* amply illustrates this point as he highlights how racial ideology became embedded in the everyday household objects and ideas of nineteenth- and twentieth-century European societies. Even today the stamp of these images remains. I am always amazed as to why White Canadians buy black caricatures as garden gnomes or household items!

Revisions of the Immigration Act that finally took place in 1962 and again in 1967 were prompted not by any major desire to further develop a "racially" pluralist society, but by interests based primarily upon economic expediency. The federal government realized that Canada would not be able to rely on its traditional source for skilled immigrants—namely Europe. It should also be recognized that in 1954, African Canadians under the banner of the Negro Citizenship Association had been able to use the growing construction of Canada as a prominent member of the Commonwealth and a co-signatory of the United Nations Declaration of Human Rights to challenge the long-standing discriminatory immigration policy.[9] This challenge, led by social and union activists, made racism in immigration policies an overt issue that non-Black Canadians could not ignore. Even after the removal of restrictions obviously based on race, the government continued to manipulate the immigration rules in favour of groups from Europe in spite of the points system and the official policy that all races be treated equally. In 1967 "five thousand immigrants passed through Toronto International Airport. Every one of the two thousand non-white immigrants was asked to post a bond. Not a single white immigrant was so asked" (Boyko 1995: 168). Canadian identity has been and continues to be constructed as White in various ways.

Black Settlers: Early Communities in Alberta

Black immigrants who made it into Alberta between 1907 and 1911 settled primarily in four isolated rural communities: Junkins, now Wildwood; Keystone, now Breton; Campsie, near Barrhead; and Amber Valley, twenty miles from Athabasca (Thakur 1988). Populated by groups who had fled persecution in Oklahoma, Amber Valley was the longest surviving Black community with its own baseball team, school and church; it was a self-contained community. According to Thakur (1988), the reason for the failure of most of these communities was the lack of infrastructural development and discrimination. These resulted in many of the settlers returning to Oklahoma and the rest resettling in Calgary or Edmonton. This group of Blacks formed the foundation of a Black population in Alberta until late 1950s/early 1960s when Blacks from the Caribbean joined them.

Although the Black settlers of Alberta arrived in Canada later than fellow Blacks in Ontario, Quebec, Nova Scotia and B.C., they faced similar prejudices and stereotypes. Common understandings of race as a biological concept were promoted in newspapers and magazines that questioned Black suitability "to the development of the highest sort of citizenship in Canada," given that their "sense of humour and predisposition to a life of ease render [their] presence undesireable." The stereotypes associated with Black women were gendered and raced. Concern was expressed about their ability to produce future citizens who would not conform to conceptions of the "Ultimate Canadian" bred of the "best stock that could be found in the world" (Cooke 1911: 11).

As in other regions in Canada, the experiences of Black pioneers in Alberta differed according to whether they settled in urban or rural areas. For those who were segregated from mainstream Canadians in self-contained rural Black communities the harsh realities of discrimination were often muted as long as they stayed within their communities. For town dwellers who had to interact with Whites on an ongoing basis, racism and discrimination were experienced daily. As with all immigrant groups, the church was an important part of Black settler life in Alberta. Churches helped maintain the culture and identity of the group and provided a social environment that was not available to them within White society. Predominantly either Methodist or Baptist, churches in Edmonton such as the Shiloh Baptist have been able to maintain a focus within the Black community. For some of these early Black pioneers, settlement meant becoming active not just within the Black community but also within the larger White-dominated community. One such community activist was Charlie King Jr. who settled in Keystone:

> Charlie would eventually become president of the Breton Farmers Union of Alberta and hold that office for many years. He believed that cooperation among farmers would improve conditions for all farmers. He and other members worked hard to establish "Farmers' Day" as a recognized holiday in Alberta. (Hooks 1997: 42)

42

Shiloh Baptist Church, Edmonton, circa 1925.

The Black Cross Nurses, Alberta. A group of nurses formed to assist the wounded soldiers who returned from World War I; 1914–1918.

Secular organizations also had a role to play in maintaining the African Canadian community. The Coloured Protective Association, formed in 1910 to fight racism in Calgary, was the foundation for other self-help organizations, such as the Universal Negro Improvement Association, the Negro Welfare Association of Alberta and the Negro Political Association, which were active up to the 1920s. While Alberta did not formally institute separate schooling, educational segregation during the early years of Black settlement resulted from geographic segregation. One publicly reported incident of the racialization of education involved Gwen Hooks whose ancestors had come from Oklahoma and settled Keystone at the turn of the century. By 1954 the composition of the town was predominantly White; most of the descendants of the original Black settlers had moved to Edmonton or Calgary. The Breton School Board, following an incident that caused racial tension in the town, refused to transfer an established Black teacher, Gwen Hooks, to a new position. Her husband Marc explains:

> It came about because of a play that Breton Drama Club staged in the school. The black community took offence because it was a parody that negatively stereotyped them. Performers with Black-ened faces employed an array of racial slurs to amuse the audience. That did not go down well with the blacks and a disturbance erupted that ended in court. (Hooks 1997: 90)

These early Black settlers in Alberta were later joined by workers and students from the Caribbean and continental Africa as immigration policies became less racialized. Ironically, the newer immigrants have come to be regarded as the "norm" in Alberta and the presence of early Black settlers has been overlooked. This denial of a Black history fits with the dominant viewpoint that Alberta was primarily created by Whites.[10]

Employment

Immigration patterns and racial ideology constructed Blacks as more suited than Whites to menial and physical labour. These low-paid jobs helped to ensure that Blacks remained at the bottom of the socio-economic ladder. Howard and Tamara Palmer suggest that in line with other cities across Canada "in Calgary during the 1920s and 1930s the job of porter was virtually the only one open to blacks" (Palmer and Palmer 1981: 10). For females in urban areas, domestic work provided a similar raced occupational specialization. Expendable and certainly returnable, Black Canadians were shunted into segmented areas of the workforce. That the porters on a train's sleeping car were all Black is an example of how, for many years, two levels of employee existed on the railways and two levels of pay

Bob Jamerson and Columbus Bowen (around 1914–18 War)
Bob Jamerson who settled in Athabaska Landing in 1910 "spent four years in Canadian forces overseas WWI 1915–19. He was with Company No 2 Construction regiment. He later joined the CPR as a porter and retired 1959" (Jamerson, Jamerson File, City Archives Edmonton).

were instituted for the same type of work so that the sleeping car conductors (all White) were higher paid. Further, sleeping car porters fit the stereotype of Blacks serving the needs of Whites. The racialization of these jobs to ensure Black workers received lower pay than fellow White workers is interesting because it illustrates a fragmentation of class interests in order to serve "race" interests. Thus the union, the Canadian Brotherhood of Railway Employees, colluded with employers, Canadian National Railroad and the Canadian Pacific Railroad, in the 1926 contract.

The deal established two job classifications. Group two was porters. Group one was everyone else. Different pay rates and benefit packages were established for the two groups. An employee's seniority and thus job security could only begin if he were in group one. Everyone in group two was forced to sign an agreement stating that they could be summarily fired and left anywhere along the line without notice or stated cause. Another stipulation was no one could change groups. (Boyko 1995: 161)

This occupational segregation was challenged by Black sleeping car porters following their organization by and affiliation with the U.S. based Brotherhood of Sleeping Car Porters. Stanley Grizzle, a union official with the Brotherhood of Sleeping Car Porters and a member of the Negro Citizenship Association, recalls the fight for employment rights:

> I was a member of the strategy team which took up the fight with the CPR for black sleeping car porters[11] to become sleeping car conductors which resulted in 1953 in the first black to be hired in this capacity on any railroad on the North American continent. (Tulloch 1975: 132)

The economic exploitation of Black women from the Caribbean, who came to Canada during the 1950s and 1960s as domestic workers, illustrates how the processes of genderization and racialization were part of immigration policies of the time. Dionne Brand's (1993) stories of these Black women in Toronto highlight how gender and race operate as interlocking forms of oppression—neither separable nor additive. Brand shows that "immigration policies have always certified men's control of women by ruling that women with spouses come as dependents" (1993: 281). However, in these gendered and racialized policies, Black women were the primary immigrant with their Black male partners coming as dependents. The result of this pattern of immigration was to construct the immigrant Black community during this period as dominated by women—a factor that affects availability of partners and consequently influences social and individual identity and continuity. This demographic imbalance seems to be a continuing trend. James Torczyner has recently found that in "the Black communities, there are substantially more women than men in the total population" with "women accounting for 52.1%, and men for 47.9% of the Black population, and respectively for 50.6% and 49.4% of the total Canadian population" (1997: 24).

Whereas the primary constructions debated by White feminists of the 1960s related to women being seen as unequal to men and tied to the home, these were not the primary constructions for Black women, particularly working-class Black women. The genderized, racialized and classed policies of the Canadian state reveal that Black women were seen as workers located outside their own homes. As such the focus of Black women's struggles against patriarchal relations were different than those of White feminists. Black women's relationship with Black men varied as they formed alliances against racism, and yet challenged them on patriarchal relations. As Brand (1993: 288) states when discussing Western society:

> Black men exhibit male-dominant behaviour and exercise influence on the ways in which Black women live, although they cannot be said to hold the same positions of power or exercise the systemic male dominance of white men. Black men are not now and never have been privy to the power structures established during slavery, colonialism, or the current configuration of capitalism.

Although we have to recognize that the political and economic pressures on Black women vary according to class and sexual orientation, we also have to recognize that Black women have the potential to act as a source of socialization for coping with racialized structures. For example, many of the students discussed in this research cited their mothers as sources who prepared them for issues of sexism and racism that they may well encounter in the wider society.

In Canada there has been a furor over the enactment of employment equity laws. Many White Canadian men and some White women have adopted a divisive "either/or" view of equity, as simply a denial of their own group. This commonsense explanation fits a social analysis of the political climate of the U.S., where as part of a process of domination, a politics of representation portrays Whites as the victims of racial inequality (Giroux 1993: 10). In the U.S. terms such as quotas, "bussing" students to schools outside their neighbourhoods, welfare and multiculturalism are used as activators to raise the insecurities and anger of Whites. Within Canadian society such activators of insecurities and criticism revolve around terms such as multiculturalism, immigration, affirmative action and political correctness. These insecurities take the form of "calls for 'colour blindness,' the opposition to affirmative action, and the claim that all that is needed is equal individual access to opportunity . . . [these support] not democratic pluralism but the perpetuation of present unequal status structures" (Yinger 1986: 33).

Figures released by Employment and Immigration Canada in 1991 reveal that the wage gap between visible minorities and other employees grew over a five-year period (*Globe and Mail*, December 30, 1992).[12] More recent statistics reveal that Black men earn 85 percent of what all Canadian men earn from full-time employment (Torczyner 1997: 36). Black women, on the other hand, earn close to the same amount as all Canadian women from full-time employment, and earn more than all Canadian women for part-time employment (Torczyner 1997: 36). However, the fact that a smaller percentage of Black persons are likely to be self-employed or employed in higher-paid occupations results in income discrepancies between Blacks and all Canadians.

Fighting for King and Country

Patriotism is an important element in the definition of who is a true Canadian and who is not—of defining who is Other. For example, during the 1914–18 war in Europe not only did the issue of conscription add to tensions between French and English Canadians, but also the issue of who would be allowed to fight for the Canadian state and under what terms became heavily racialized.

James Walker charts the battle that Canadians of non-British origins had to undertake in order to be recognized as having a right to fight. The ideology of empire was used to construct and determine the ways in which army life and enlistment became racialized:

> Science and public opinion accepted that certain identifiable groups lacked the valour, discipline, and intelligence to fight a modern war. Since those same groups were also the subjects of the European overseas empires, prudence warned that a taste of killing white men might serve as appetizer should they be enlisted against a European enemy. (Walker 1989: 1)

For African Canadians in all provinces, no official policies of exclusion were formulated for enlistment but, as with the immigration policies at the turn of the twentieth century, racism operated at a subtle level. Similar to patterns of settlement, the number of Blacks wanting to mix with Whites was crucial. Thus, where an individual officer permitted, individual Blacks might be allowed to join a unit and thus see active service.

The issue of racism, and the racialization of the army, was not tackled directly by the government. Instead it stated that no official policy prevented the enlistment of soldiers of African descent. As early as 1914, African Canadians in North Buxton were complaining to Ottawa of racial exclusion and seeking corrective action from the government. As usual the government responded with the official policy and chose to ignore concrete acts of racism. In response to a question in the House of Commons on March 24, 1916, the government insisted that "there is not Dominion legislation authorizing discrimination against coloured people," and the militia was able to state that "'no regulations' or restrictions prevented the enrolment of coloured men who possess the 'necessary qualifications'" (Walker 1989: 5).

In addition to the empire ideology being a factor in racializing the recruitment experience, many generals adhered to a biological definition of race and believed in the inherent inferiority of African Canadians, "civilized" or not. Thus, General Gwatkin reported to the Militia Council in 1916: "[T]he civilised negro is vain and imitative; in Canada he is not being impelled to enlist by a high sense of duty; and the average white man will not associate with him on terms of equality" (cited in Boyko 1995: 159). The final solution to the barriers placed before African Canadian recruits was a segregated army permitted by Prime Minister Borden. Number 2 Battalion (Coloured) consisted of African Canadians, but all officers were White—an arrangement that reinforced the idea that African Canadians could not organize themselves. They were allocated jobs that required physical labour, such as building bridges, digging trenches and clearing roads. These tasks contributed to the war effort, but the battalion did not engage in frontline activity.[13] In the European war of 1939–45 units were formally desegregated, but in some units African Canadian soldiers continued to eat, associate and socialize only with fellow Blacks. It is also worth noting that the Air Force and the Navy were even more reluctant to allow Blacks to integrate, and when they did agree to involve Blacks these privileged few were rarely allowed into the elite units.

The importance of who fights for whom and under what terms they can display patriotism comes to represent part of the construction and racialization of who can be seen as a true Canadian. Whether we like it or not, part of the process of othering surrounding issues such as whether Sikhs should be able to wear a turban in British Legion Halls in Alberta is the ability of "White" groups to construct soldiers "who gave their all for this country" as White—as one of "us" rather than one of "them."

BUT ISN'T THAT IN THE PAST?
AREN'T WE ALL JUST ETHNIC GROUPS?

In modern day Canada, racialism and racism are able to operate in the shadow of the common belief that our country is humane, benevolent, hospitable and modern—all qualities that can be held up as proof against the possibility of intolerance and discrimination (Schick 1995). The use of Whiteness as a reference point for Canadian identity and the invisibility of this approach leads to the maintenance of White dominance. We have to recognize that the process of marginalization itself is

> central to the formation of the dominant culture. The first and very important stage is . . . to recognize the cultural and political category of Whiteness. It seems obvious to say it but in practice the racialization of our social order is only recognized in relation to racialized "others." (Carby, cited in Giroux 1993: 131)

Whites within society do not have their ethnicity made apparent. For many Whites, ethnicity is something that belongs to someone else (and is something that Whites can purchase via dress, diet and dance). Radical theorists postulate that when White identity loses its transparency and the apparent "racelessness" that accompanies racial domination, "whiteness becomes a matter of anxiety and concern and its dominance becomes visible" (McCarthy and Crichlow 1993: 8). In Canadian society this process is more complex since there is an emphasis on everyone belonging to an ethnic group. Where the similarities arise is in discussions as to the component of ethnic identity. Thus some individuals will declare that they have no distinct culture, and nothing to show, as compared to the more exotic nature of the Others.

As part of current racialization processes in Canada, the term "ethnicity" has acquired new currency in the creation and promotion of dominance. Ethnicity is seen as a direct replacement for the term "race," one that fits more neatly with our modern liberal sensibilities; many advocate dropping "race" and using "ethnicity." The Canadian state, as legally multicultural, promotes the term ethnicity to refer to differences within society based on geographic origins and the process of immigration. With the eschewing of the term race, ethnic divisions come to seem plausible, adequate and commonsensical as the term ethnicity assumes a complacent "innocence." Yet in reality any construct that entails categories should be suspect since it has the potential to create hierarchies and therefore dominance. As with race, ethnicity is an ideological construct that is used for analysis and as such is problematic. Not recognizing ethnicity allows racism to operate as cultural oppression or, to use Chris Mullard's (1986) term, ethnicism. Ethnicism is an ideology that explicitly proclaims the existence of "multiethnic" equality but implicitly presupposes an ethnic or cultural hierarchical order (Mullard 1986). Ethnicism is thus able to

> define the experience of racialized groups in culturalist terms: that is, it posits ethnic "difference" as the primary modality around which social life is constituted and experienced. Cultural needs are defined largely as independent of other social experiences centred around class, gender, racism or sexuality. That means that a group identified as culturally different is assumed to be internally homogenous. (Brah 1992: 129)

It is important to bear in mind that definitions and meanings associated with both ethnicity and race are social constructions that shift constantly, reflecting the changing dynamics of gender, race/ethnic and political relations over time (Ng 1993: 185). Although various definitions of ethnicity indicate that the concept includes a racial dimension (Gordon 1964: 24), these aspects are often suppressed in order to accent cultural dimensions. For those of European descent, culture and/or religions are often primary differentiating factors; therefore, the emphasis on culture does suit peoples originating in Europe. However, this categorization, with its Eurocentric focus, results in immigrant experiences being analyzed within a framework and model developed to account for the migratory experiences of Europeans (Omi and Winant 1986: 20).

Today the process of othering takes on a different shape and at present draws on and conflates the terms race, culture and nation to facilitate movement towards a newer form of racism. This new form, similar to ethnicism, innocently highlights the naturalness of the physical and cultural differences between us, but then proceeds to argue that it is human nature to cling to one's own kind, one's culture and one's nation (Barker 1981). What this leads to is a simplistic rationalization of the exclusion of those who look physically different or who are culturally different. The rationalization is no longer directly based on the old coding of race, but on an allegedly universal human nature that is nepotistic and that seeks to preserve its own national way of life (de Lepervanche and Bottomley 1988: 2). So we find that this new racism is produced as part of a general political move that aligns "race" with national and cultural belonging.

In England this "new cultural racism" has the ability to "link patriotism, nationalism, xenophobia, Englishness, Britishness, militarism and gender into a complex which gives 'race' its contemporary meaning" (Gilroy 1991: 43). In Canadian society examples of similar linkages within "new cultural racism," alongside biological racism, can be found in the rhetoric of some Alberta Reform Party politicians such as Bob Ringma. For him, biological racism is still relevant, thus making it still perfectly acceptable to put "Blacks" at the back of the shop if their visual presence offends customers. Unfortunately, Alberta is not alone in exhibiting this new form of cultural racism. Comments by Jacques Parizeau following the loss of the Quebec referendum illustrate further how othering based on culture and national belonging becomes intertwined with Quebec politics. For Parizeau, defeat was partly due to the "ethnic vote," a challenge that posits "ethnic groups" as interlopers—not the "pure laine"—who have no right to participate in a referendum on the future of Quebec. Similarly, Bouchard's comment that not enough White Francophone babies were being born indicates that Blacks can never be seen as truly belonging to Quebec regardless of their culture, language or place of birth. They just are not "pure laine," itself a mystical concept that ignores in particular First Nations presence in Quebec society.

The nation-state can thus be seen as the central organizing unit of culture and nationalism, with culture acting as a reactive force that allows the drawing of boundaries (Wallerstein 1991). This link between cultures and the drawing of boundaries is observable in present-day Canada in the conflict between those who want the state to officially advocate the maintenance of distinct cultural identities and those who believe that to be

Canadian is to be assimilated into a common identity. To be a true national requires subsuming one's own identity to that which is dictated by a dominant group. Hence, within Canada the conflicting perspectives about hyphenated Canadians—as exemplified by the public's reception of Neil Bissoondath's (1994) book *Selling Illusions*—are symbolic of a deeper conflict concerning ethnic identity. Bissoondath's arguments "are mainly constructed around dismissing the claims that people of colour make concerning various forms of domination" (Walcott 1997: 79). It is interesting to see the parallels in general society between the romantic constructions of "Englishness" used to exclude and attack the Black presence in England and the romantic construction of "Canadian" taking place in Canada in order to support the marginalization of non-White groups. "If nationalism is an ideology of the first person plural, who tells 'us' who 'we' are, then it is also an ideology of the third person. There cannot be an 'us' without a 'them'" (Billig 1995: 78). Linked to a definition of "us" and "them" and the process of othering is the issue of "whiteness." Used as a reference point for Canadian identity, the invisibility of this approach leads to the maintenance of White dominance.

REPRESENTATION

Representation is the social process of making sense within all available signifying systems: speech, writing, print and video (Hartley 1994: 267). The process of representing promotes images of people in wider society. This process becomes implicated in defining the "us" and the "them" in society. We need to remember that representation and reality are concepts that determine and are determined by each other. People do not act or view the world in a certain way because they are Black, women or working class; they do so because they are raced, gendered, and classed and because their experiences are constructed socially both by themselves and by others (Levinson 1992: 220).

Stereotypes, however inaccurate, are one form of representation. Like fictions they are created to serve as substitutions, standing in for what is real. They do not tell it like it is, but invite and encourage pretence (hooks 1992). Stereotypes abound when there is distance. They are an invention, an understanding that one has when the steps that would make real knowing possible cannot be taken, or are not allowed (hooks 1992: 170). Often stereotypes formulated in Canada draw on the United States for reinforcement. If we look specifically at Toronto, Andre Alexis suggests that intellectually there is a strong alignment with the United States and that Blacks are conceptualized as a phenomenon from the United States that has crept north or emigrated from Africa. The problem that results from this view of Black Canadians is that a specific form of Black American identity is portrayed as a universal identity for all Blacks:

> Canada is *often* invisible in American writing, black Canada even more so, and it seems to me that black Canadians react to that invisibility in at least two ways. One way is to assume that we *are* all included in definitions of "New World Africa" reality, that Canada is America (but *pianissimo*) and that bell hooks and Derrick Bell are speaking about (louder) versions of our experience. The other way is by trying to sing, dance or write Canada for ourselves, to define our own terrain and situation. (Alexis 1995: 17, original emphasis)

The "writing of our own terrain" encouraged by Alexis is problematic in an age when the growth and acceleration of economic and cultural networks occurs on a worldwide scale and basis. These economic and cultural networks have accelerated the flow of cultures across geographical, political and cultural borders. The result is that communication technologies, from print to digital pulses, make particular ways of dressing and behaving possible internationally and the ability to define our own terrain less plausible.

The spread of technology has increased the importance of popular culture in terms of its ability to offer identities and representations to a wider audience. Thus, popular culture has been one forum through which mainstream White culture has been able to establish an ideological framework of symbols, concepts and images that influences how we understand, interpret and represent "racial differences" (Omi 1989: 114). Thus films, particularly those about working-class urban males, music videos and compact discs provide ways for society to understand Black lives and experiences.

Representations of primarily North American Black experiences can be read in a variety of ways. In addition to offering Black youths spaces for identification, films such as "Menace II Society" and "Boyz N the Hood" are readily digested by young Whites. These films become sources for White society to vicariously come to know Black youths. "Media has become a substitute for experience, and what constitutes understanding is grounded in a decentred and diasporic world of difference, displacement and negotiations" (Giroux 1996: 33). These films attempt to account for the economic and social conditions that generate a specific type of Black masculinity, but they often fail. As Njeri (1993: 34) highlights, "[U]nfortunately, the black male-as-menace film genre often fails to artfully tie this nihilism to its poisonous roots in America's system of inequality. And because this fails to do so, the effects of these toxic forces are seen as causes." While some youths are able to locate the roots of such male constructions and representations by reflecting on their own experiences, there is no uniformity in people's readings of the film text. Thus for many suburban middle-class Whites youths who may have no understanding of the economic and social environment from which these Black masculinities emerge, the reading is one of exoticism and further reinforcement of Black male stereotypes.

The popular media of newspapers and television also provide a means for social groups to get to know each other and, therefore, are a source for stereotypes and representation of African Canadians. One of the most evocative sources of images of young Black men are rap records and music videos, developed to appeal to affective and gendered constructions. However, it is not just music that plays a role in creating the image of young Black men as an alien threat; print media and news commentaries are also implicated. Deborah Britzman's (1991: 93) analysis of news commentaries demonstrates such a connection and illustrates that in these contradictory commentaries, "Blacks are never victims, white men are never raced, black masculinity is always criminalized, white women are perpetually victimized, and black woman are irrelevant." Thus we need to recognize, as Himani Bannerji suggests, that newspapers and television programs are

> cultural lenses through which communities are viewed and introduced to each other literally via media. Mis- or dis-information crowd the news and other television programmes, while the fashion industry, sports and music equate black people with the body and the natural gift for rhythm, and the Chinese with an innate propensity to do well in mathematics (1995: 155).

Analysis of the present day immigration debates reveals the role that newspapers play in the construction of certain citizens as acceptable—essentially those who are White. Carole Schick (1995) argues that the media presents a "white-skin subjectivity" as an identifying characteristic in Canadian national identity. Non-Whites are seen as being at odds with the constructed White subject, they are not considered Canadian. An example is provided by the question often posed by those who see a Canadian as of European descent: "So where are you *really* from?" Another example of this denial of acceptance of Black youths is the policy of "repatriating" criminals of African Canadian origin to countries that they have not known since early childhood. As recently as August 1997 the Jamaican government complained about the Canadian government's practice of deporting to Jamaica criminals who have had their criminal skills honed and developed within Canadian society.

THE USE OF HISTORY TO CHALLENGE THE PRESENT

The importance of investigating how the process of racialization has occurred in Canadian society is twofold. First, history plays an important role in the formation and interpretation of culture and identity. Second, even though history is often written from the victors' viewpoint and used to reinforce dominance, it still has the ability to act as a form of resistance to domination in present-day society.

In recent years, radical social theorists have moved from a position that stressed the dominance of structures in determining behaviour towards a viewpoint that recognizes the complexity of resistance to dominance. This resistance to dominance and racialization is clearly shown by the ways in which African Canadians developed social, religious and political organizations to challenge and contest the various stereotypes that existed. In the 1940s social activists working with groups such as the sleeping car porters in Alberta found that social issues concerning Black Canadians extended beyond the initial confines of employment equity on the railways to issues of racism in job placements and public accommodation.[14] On a more widespread level, this activism on the part of the Black Canadian community in conjunction with sympathetic Whites heralded the onset of various pieces of anti-discrimination legislation during the post 1929–45 European war period. Although it was and is difficult to maintain a cohesive activist front and a Black Canadian identity, when faced with differences based on geographic origins, gender, class, religion and regions, the Black community was able to finally form a National Black Coalition in 1969.

In line with this recognition of resistance have been theoretical developments suggesting that historical social memory can aid the development of radicalism. For example, Canadian historical interpretation marginalizes the presence of African Canadians by omitting their lived experiences. Recognition of this marginality can alert those who are attuned to such omissions to question why this should be so—opening up the possibility of a critique of present day domination. For the youths in this book who adopt a more overt and radical stance on issues related to a Black identity, this is a factor that comes into play. For these students locating oneself in the margins can be a strategy of empowerment:

> by locating oneself within the margins, one refuses to forget the past and instead keeps it alive in memory. When memory is politicized, the margins come to represent a social location that is on the one hand a place of "deprivation" and on the other hand a particular way of seeing reality whose intent is survival and resistance. (Hudak 1993: 174)

Thus, "historical memory rejects the notion of the past as a linear progression, history as an unproblematic event moving forward toward greater heights of achievement and progress" (Giroux and Trend 1992: 68). In this scenario a countermemory can be used as a source of resistance. The importance of this process is that "since memory is actually a very important factor in struggle . . . if one controls people's memory, one controls their dynamism. And one controls their experience, their knowledge of previous struggles" (Foucault, cited in O'Farrell 1989: 92).

If we define culture as the lived experiences of people then it is important to analyze how those lived experiences intersect with the social, political and economic climate of specific periods in history since "people are trapped in history, and history is trapped in them" (Baldwin, cited in Philip 1992: 229). That people make history is undeniable, but often the history that they make is contained and confined by political and economic constraints. What this historical overview reveals is that the history of African Canadians, as with other groups, is racialized; thus the ways in which subjects were able to interact with others within society often depended upon raced meanings and expectations attached to their behaviour. The fact that those of African descent were perceived as being of a different species, as indolent, lazy and lascivious, affected their choice of occupation, where they lived and with whom they were able to socialize.

In the present day, our identities have changed from Negro through Coloured to Black, and now are moving on to African Canadians. Although the descriptors have changed and the ways in which representations are constructed have changed with the growth in new technology, the underlying stereotypes about our behaviour and attitudes seem strangely familiar. Thus, as the historical overview indicates, African Canadians were never perceived by the Anglo or Francophone elite as part of the Canadian landscape or mosaic. Constructed as alien to and deviant from what the dominant group views as Canadian, those of African descent born in Canada can recognize to this day this continuing othering in the question, "Where are you *really* from?"

NOTES

1. See Crawford Killan's *Go Do Some Great Thing: The Black Pioneers of British Columbia* (1978) and James Pilton's master's thesis *Negro Settlement in British Columbia* (1951) for in-depth discussions of these issues.
2. Buxton Mission School, opened in 1850 and funded by the Presbyterian church, was an exception to the various forms of segregated schooling. Integrated, but primarily Black, with a curriculum that offered Greek and Latin as well as religion, the school saw its mandate as one of training for the professions and trades (Alexander and Glaze 1996: 71).
3. As well as being the first woman editor in North America, Mary Anne Shadd

was an advocate of women's rights and a community activist. There is a discussion of Mary Ann Shadd's life in Bristow et al., *We're Rooted Here and They Can't Pull Us Up: Essays in African Canadian Women's History* (1994: 161).

4. For further discussion of True Band Societies see Walker 1980: 118. Other organizations such as the Reform Benevolent Society, Chatham 1853 and the Windsor Ladies Club 1854 were formed by and for Black women in the community. These organizations, often with a classed dimension reinforced by a strong moral and religious element, played a role in the collective "racial uplift" of Blacks.

5. Blacks protested the petition and challenged the canvassers. As the *Edmonton Bulletin* reported, "[O]ne canvasser's steps were dogged by several negroes who intruded into the conversation and canvassed and sought to dissuade the latter from signing" (cited in Thomson 1979).

6. The *Bulletin*, which had an association with Immigration Minister Frank Oliver, was in this specific example more restrained and discrete in its public denouncements of Black immigration.

7. The uninvited races were the "Chinies- the Hindoes- and the Japs" (Arthur Fortin, cited in Shepard 1991: 28).

8. The reciprocity agreement was drafted in 1911 between Canada and the United States. It allowed "the free entry of most natural products and set lower rates on a number of commodities, including agricultural implements" (Finkel et al. 1993: 292).

9. The campaign of this Negro Citizenship Association revealed unity as well as splits in the Black community. While the predominantly Black churches did not overtly support the delegation, the other more mainstream organizations such as the United Church and the Canadian Labour Conference did offer support (Alexander and Glaze 1996: 175–78).

10. This viewpoint is represented by the comments of Susan Ruttan (1998) in her article in the *Edmonton Journal:* "But here in Alberta, how much black history is there, really?" and "given our lack of black history . . ." (February 14, I2).

11. The wives of porters became active in the auxiliaries of the Brotherhood, extending the new politicization into community organizing and education.

12. Margaret Philp points out in the *Globe and Mail* (February 18, A3) that in the public sector during March 1987, 4.7 percent of employees were visible minorities, a level falling far short of the Treasury Board's goal of 9 percent.

13. Among the volunteers for the European war of 1914–18 were Billy and Arthur Ware, sons of John Ware, the famous late nineteenth-century and early twentieth-century Alberta cowboy. In Velma Carter and Wanda Akili's book, *The Window of Our Memories* (1981), their sister Nettie Ware recalls that "both my brothers came home; they fought in trenches in those times, in World War I. Then Billy died with tuberculosis; he was buried in the Field of Honor in Calgary" (1981: 82). For a more thorough discussion and veteran accounts of the Number 2 Battalion, please see Calvin Ruck's *The Black Battalion* (1987).

14. For example, union organizer A. Randolph Philips and T.S. King are attributed with organizing in 1947 the Alberta Association for the Advancement of Coloured Peoples to fight discrimination in Calgary.

CHAPTER THREE

SOURCES FOR IDENTITIES

Jimmy: *Most of them [rappers] make sense, you learn about stuff,
talk about Black and White . . . . Most of them are racist though.*
Jennifer: *[What do you mean] when you say racist?*
Jimmy: *They'll sing racist songs, but that's the way they feel. They
probably face more than me, living in the States with Black and
White.*

For the African Canadian students who share their experiences in this book,
photographic, televisual and aural images act as sources for the identities
they adopt in their school lives and adolescence. These various images offer
a concept of Blackness with which African Canadian youth can experiment.
These cultural images interact with class, gender and family structures.
Films, music and sports provide potential sources of identity, as well as
sources for the creation and reinforcement of stereotypes. Identities expressed in concrete ways through dress and style have racially constructed
elements that affect interpersonal relations with other raced groups in
school.

Films

Films such as "Menace II Society" and "Boyz N the Hood," which portray
the nihilistic lifestyle of urban African American youths in conjunction
with the violence and despair that envelops that life, are well known among
the students interviewed. These films give many of the students knowledge
as well as a vicarious experience of life in the urban areas of the United
States. Some see the urban decay portrayed as being central to Black lives
while peripheral for the majority of Whites. This seems to reinforce the
dichotomy of "them" and "us"; it strengthens the students' association with
Blacks in the ghetto and their sense that White Americans are set apart and
disinterested.

Toni: *It's the Black people who want to talk about it [the condition
of Blacks in urban areas], not the Whites, because they [Blacks]*

58

want to solve it . . . . It's movies like "Menace II Society," "Boyz N' the Hood" that made people realize what's going on.

For others, viewing films such as "Menace II Society" is not only vicarious but in a sense cathartic, in that viewing the conditions that exist in the U.S. results in a stronger identification with Canadian society. Such films provide the opportunity for African Canadians to be grateful that the society they live in is different from that portrayed on the screen.

Bob:*"[Menace II Society]" . . . portrayed life like what it was in L.A. . . . it's car jacking, sticking people up with guns . . . . Here it's totally different, so we get to see what they do, and how it's different for them and us and what we could do not to be like that.*

Many of the participants in my research indicated an awareness not only of Blacks in America, but also of fellow Blacks in other parts of the world. Some of the students indicated how their race and the dynamics of geopolitics often determine the economic and social conditions of Black people. With regard to Southern Africa students comment:

Toni: *They [Whites] come in, rule for 200 years and then leave and say, "Now you rule." . . . Even though it's not my problem, you can't help but care.*

Lorraine: *It makes me so upset that so many people had to sacrifice themselves for this day [when Blacks were allowed to vote in South Africa].*

The depth of knowledge that many of the students displayed reflects in some ways the popular icons determined by White mainstream culture as much as by Black culture. By this I mean that the two Black individuals that the students most often identified as people they would like to know more about were Malcolm X and Nelson Mandela. Both of these men had recently been given a lot of publicity in the mainstream media: Malcolm X via the Spike Lee film of that name, and Nelson Mandela in the run-up to the South African elections. The students were aware that their knowledge was limited and that they relied on films and other sources for information:

Joy: *If it wasn't for the movie about Malcolm X, I'd know nothing . . . . I read the book "Roots". . . that's all I know.*

Ida: *Like with Malcolm X, I didn't really know much about him, so*

I wanted to find out more. Now I know [after watching the film].

Roy: *People came to our church and were asking questions about poets [and other Black people] and I didn't know much. . . . I know about Booker T. Washington, that's obvious stuff but not others . . . . My parents started teaching me but that's the only place I can get it.*

As part of the process of using films to garner information about Black subjects, the students highlighted the fact that the mainstream cinema corporations often control access to and availability of the films. Films specifically about the Black community are mainly shown for a short period of time and predominantly at one location in Edmonton. White-dominated society is directly involved in making available to young Blacks representations of themselves that aid in the construction of their identity. This availability relates to Stuart Hall's (1991a; 1991b) point that the culture of a given ethnic group is not created in a vacuum, but is often in relation to of the dominant society.

Although films about the Black community provide sources of knowledge and a potential base for the construction of a Black identity, often this "knowledge" is not accepted in a simplistic manner. A few of the male students indicated an awareness of how some movies they watched were in fact undermining the identity of Black people and portraying them as peripheral, expendable and reliant upon the Whites [usually males] to solve their problems:

Eldridge: *The [films] always show that the Black man is always saved by White people. We can never save ourselves, I can't understand that. We do stuff for ourselves, but they always show the White man trying to save the Black person.*

Nelson: *Kung fu Joe [a Black guy] was the first one killed [in a film]. The White guy never got touched.*

Television

The media often filters knowledge about Black communities as well as existing subcultures. As Hebdige suggests, "[M]uch of what finds itself encoded in subculture has already been subjected to a certain amount of handling by the media" (1979: 85).

Canadian television is dominated by programs developed for and by the U.S. market that tend to depict constructions of "life" in the U.S. These programs have a strong impact and powerful influence on all youths. Black youths ingest the offerings of a predominantly Eurocentric lifestyle, as well as programs attempting to portray the lives of Black families and individuals. Many of the students indicated an awareness of themselves not just as Canadians but also as Blacks. They watched "Fresh Prince of Bel Air," a situation comedy portraying the life of a Black family, not only because it was funny and they could relate to it but also because they saw it as depicting Black people in a positive way.

The students mentioned re-runs of programs such as "North and South" and "Roots"; many found that these programs were emotional, and that they seemed to add to and reinforce a "collective memory"[1] of being Black. As Toni, who watched the serial "North and South," stated,

> *[she] wanted to put [her] hand in the television set and wring the White man's neck.*

These programs seem to give the students an inkling of what the past entailed for their forebears. They also provide an opportunity for the students to reinforce their group identity as Black people. Toni gives an example of this process in discussing her parent's reaction to Roots:

> *my parents have prejudice towards [White] people especially after watching "Roots."*

Alongside re-runs of historical serials, talk shows endlessly sift through the issue of "Black" identity and have a voyeuristic appeal to both Black and White audiences as issues such as inter-racial marriages and the self-identity of mixed-race individuals emerge as topics of discussion. As part of this scenario and "crossover"[2] appeal, the Oprah Winfrey show was mentioned several times by the students. In affirmation of this point, a July 1994 edition of the *Edmonton Journal* noted the impact that the show had on the book-buying public of North America. Further, it alluded to the number of people who watched the show and listened to the opinions that the Black host articulated. In general, the format of "Oprah" and other talk shows provides not only entertainment for the students, but also a catalyst for discussion of racial issues among friends at school. Illustrative of this was a heated debate during one focus group session in which some students held various perspectives about a participant on a television show who was denying her Blackness and wanting to be seen as White.

News programs also play a role in the construction of Black identity. They select and relay news of other areas of the world, and highlight and universalize the behaviour of individual Blacks to all Blacks.[3]

MUSIC

Music was important to some students not only for entertainment, but because it sometimes acted as a catalyst for their social lives. It provided meanings and themes with which the students could identify, and indicated adherence to their raced origins. For many of the students interviewed—with the exception of those who were heavily involved in church-based activities—music was a focus of their socializing outside school and an indirect form of *boundary maintenance*[4] for the Black group.

The students listened to a wide variety of music produced predominantly by Black musicians. Soul and rhythm and blues were mentioned frequently by the students, especially the group "Jodeci" by the young women, who indicated that the words were "good and powerful." Some of the Black students did not automatically relate to the type of music played on the school radio systems. In both schools, individual Black students were involved in attempting to broaden the type of music played over the school intercom to include rhythm and blues and rap, which were seen as appealing to the tastes of some Black students. These attempts by the students to achieve musical representation of their cultural backgrounds were not always acceptable to the mainstream non-Black audiences however:

> Bobby: *For the music it's pure "bala" music. They [non-Black] play, like, rocker music.*

> Nelson: *I want to hear something like R&B, or slow music. They are playing alternative.*

> Gary: *I was on the radio station once every two weeks .... I played stuff like rap and R&B and people kept coming up and complaining. "How come you don't play this and you don't play that." I told them that "All the other thirteen days you are getting what you want. This day is for what I want to play and hear." . . . Eventually the teacher started buying country CDs and rock CDs [thereby supporting the status quo].*

> Roy: *[We got involved with the school radio because] it seemed that our music wasn't represented.*

Reggae was generally popular, particularly among those with an affinity with Jamaica. One of the friendship groups established at Valley High was based around a reggae "sound system" that played at parties. Thus the music, friendship and school were intertwined for some students, enhancing a closer bond.

For some of the students rap music and hip-hop culture had acquired a signification of "roughness" and "Blackness," which was seen as reflecting the lives of young disaffected Black youths in the urban areas of the U.S. It was interesting that some students perceived a similarity between "rap" and "reggae." This similarity was based not so much on the beat but more on the social content of the songs and the style in which the lyrics were communicated to their audience. Links were made between the two musical forms in 1979 by *New Musical Express*, a British music newspaper, which noted that "the deejay who raps does not appear to be a million miles removed from the ancient Jamaican art of toasting" (cited in George 1992: 17). The lyrics of some reggae songs reinforce the views espoused by rap songs, namely the tough "gangsta" image:

> Desmond: *We don't see ourselves as "bad." But everyone wants a rough gangster "look" . . . a serious guy who nobody wants to mess with. Everybody see him, and he'll get respect, or "big up," as we'd say in Jamaica. A lot of Jamaican songs talk about "gangster" and "bitch" and all that.*

This linking of the musical forms among Jamaicans and Blacks in the United States and to some extent Britain reflects the movement of descendants of the Black diaspora—the geographical scattering of those of African descent as a result of the slave trade. What we see is affirmation that culture is not static but adapts and changes with the structure of the society it encounters and with which it interacts. Dick Hebdige indicates such a trend when he outlines the move made by rap disc jockey Kool Herc from Jamaica to the United States in 1967 and the accompanying changes in the presentation of his musical form (1987: 139).

Some students indicated that they identified with the social content of what the rappers had to say. It deepened the youths' understanding of and empathy with the rappers and their understanding of how they react to the despair and violence they face in their daily lives:

> Toni: *In the States, in the ghetto . . . those people rap about what they know and if you want to stop the "gangsta" rap and what they are saying then go into the projects and help!*

> Lorraine: *They [rappers] are talking about people getting shot everyday, people who are their friends, their families. They grow up with helicopters flying overhead, with the fear they are going to get shot. I feel so sorry for them . . . but they have to live like that, they have to do it to survive.*

63

Toni: *It's [rap's] like a window.*

Lorraine: *America doesn't like people to see it.*

Other students, while agreeing that rap was an accurate critique of the conditions in the ghetto, nonetheless felt that there were negative aspects to it. Some saw rappers as individuals cashing in on the plight of poor Blacks in the ghettos, and often not having anything new or radical to say other than to advocate "shooting up people." Rappers were seen as portraying negative roles for young Black men. Both males and females felt that some of the young men at school had to act tough in order to portray a "bad" or "rough" image. Some students expressed concern that in constructing an identity around rappers and characters portrayed in films, many young Black men were in fact reinforcing the negative stereotypes that already existed about them; they were becoming part of the process that creates these stereotypes. However, one of the strengths of rap's ability to attract young men is identified by Nelson George:

> [T]he great thing about rap for its early audience was that it created home-grown heroes with larger-than-life persona. Shaft, Truck Turner, and Nigger Charlie were disposable Hollywood fictions. Grandmaster Flash, Afrika Bambaataa and Kurtis Blow were stars of the ghetto. (1992: 5)

Part of the "bad" image that rap has developed derives from its negative portrayal of women. Some of the young women revealed that they felt that the music was insulting and misogynist in its constant objectification of women as "hoes" (whores) and "bitches":

> Toni: *Snoop [Doggy Dogg] is disrespectful to women by calling them bitches. I don't think they should be disrespectful to their own people when your people are being brought down by outside forces [mainstream White society].*

> Rosa: *It's a kind of stereotype that's put on rappers, they have to live up to. And White people and the Black people create it, and it becomes a fad. For them [rappers] to make their million dollars they have to go up there and cuss and bitch and shoot up. They have to live up to it; it's like a cycle that keeps going and going.*

> Pearl: *I think that people should to be able to see a difference between reality and make-believe. Some of those things in rap is true, but that doesn't mean that you have to go out and do it. It's*

not everything that you see that you do.

Lorraine: *It's our culture, the beat and the words but others make it into a fad.*

George: *But [we have to ask ourselves] who is it that owns the records? It's the people who own the records. It's the people who are behind Snoop Doggy Dogg, that are pushing him that give rap people a bad turn. If you don't know it don't listen to it, because you won't understand.*

Milton: *Sometimes it's as if he [Snoop Doggy Dogg] has nothing to say. There is nothing to say other than he is going to shoot someone in the head.*

Even though these students felt that rap's message had been commodified (Koza 1994), they felt that rap still had the potential to teach them about themselves:

Jimmy: *Most of them [rappers] make sense, you learn about stuff, talk about Black and White . . . . Most of them are racist though.*

Jennifer: *[What do you mean] when you say racist?*

Jimmy: *They'll sing racist songs, but that's the way they feel. They probably face more than me, living in the States with Black and White.*

This charge of racism applied to rap music stems from the rappers urging violence against Whites. However, while the music may reveal dislike of Whites and other raced groups, it does not seem to demonstrate racism in the sense of the ability to assert power, and therefore dominance (Elliott and Fleras 1992). This distinction between racism and prejudice is important and complex, and it underlies the contentions as to whether Black people can be racist towards Whites.[5] In a different vein, rap can act as a potential source for cognitive dissonance for some of the students who had White family members and saw rap lyrics as advocating the killing of White people.

Bob: *They [rappers] always talk about making a difference, kill the White people, on and on and on . . . . They say White people is always prejudiced, but I notice it's us too that's prejudiced. It's not just us, like every other race is prejudiced against one race .*

. . . If we portray it in our music like that, it's just going to cause trouble. Especially saying kill all the White people, 'cause some of my family are White.

COMMUNITY SOURCES

Parents and relatives and the wider Black community are also sources of identity for Black youths. For example, one student's parent belonged to a book club that sold literature about Black people. Another student was involved in the activities her relatives organized as members of a Black women's group. Other students had joined specific Black youth organizations. Many of the youths disseminated newly acquired knowledge to other students within the school community.

Grace: *Last year I was able to teach people stuff about Steve Biko.*

Kathleen: *If it was your own culture . . . you would work so much harder. When I did that Black history project . . . I sacrificed my homework . . . because I was so excited . . . involved. You feel so much better. You walk away thinking, "Yeah we did this we did that." You want to brag. I would go to school and say, "Did you know?"* (Chorus of agreement and laughter, as the rest of the group remember and agree with her comment.)

Lorraine: *I looked through* Race and Sex *[a book].*

Toni: *[Don't forget] you're supposed to bring that for me [to read].*

Lorraine: *My Dad sends away for . . . books that you don't see around . . . he'll order them from the States.*

Within the wider Black community, churches often act as sources of knowledge and places where a degree of autonomy from White society and freedom to exercise control over their own lives can be achieved.[6] Dionne Brand (1991), in discussing the role that churches played in the lives of Black women in Ontario between 1920 and the 1950s, suggests a complex interplay between gender and race. Although "women were not found in positions of power in the Black church, they were certainly to be found in traditional positions of responsibility" (1991: 18). Churches offer Black youth alternative meanings and understandings of themselves and society by offering them "a chance not to be elsewhere, not to be in other places still open at all hours of the night, not to be in those places that expose them to temptation" (Foster 1996: 58). These alternative positions often contradict those positions offered by the musical and televisual media, which is prominent in Black youth culture. Ken Pryce describes the role that Black churches play in providing alternative identities for Black youth in Britain:

> The strength of the West Indian church in Britain is no doubt due to the fact that, as all-black, self-segregating organizations based on solidarity among members, they have remained impenetrable to all attempts by the state to whitewash and subdue West Indian institutions with its policy of multiculturalism and integration. (1979: 273)

Students also made mention of classes they attended on weekends. These were organized by the Black community and provided the students with extra help with the official curriculum and access to knowledge of history created by Blacks as a social group. Again this form of knowledge was shared with others.

STEREOTYPES

Stereotypes are generally used to readily categorize a complex array of information. "Applied to race and ethnic relations, stereotypes refer to a shared consensus regarding the generalized attributes of others with respect to perceived physical or cultural characteristics" (Elliott and Fleras 1992: 335). Some students indicated that seeing themselves as a group was not only dependent upon self-ascription, but also upon how others viewed them in society. Commonality of social experiences in a White-dominated society emerges as an important aspect of defining what it is to be Black:

> Jennifer: *What do Black people have in common?*

> Toni: *Experiences with the White man.*

> Lorraine: *We've all been there.*

Indicated here are the two main perspectives as to why unity along ethnic and racial lines is maintained. Students suggested that others often viewed them in and out of school in stereotypical terms as Black. One of the teachers also was of this opinion:

> Ms. Eraser: *We have more Black kids in the school than we have ever had . . . . I think Black people are becoming quite visible now,*

and I'm not very sure it's terribly positive the way that they are becoming visible.

A few individuals within the schools saw Black students as being physically alike to such an extent that they were indistinguishable from one another. In one school two young women described how on their first encounter with one teacher he indicated that he not only viewed them as potential "troublemakers," but also suggested that he would not be able to tell them apart even though they looked "nothing alike." For many students this matter of teachers not being willing or able to distinguish one Black person from another can be annoying as well as detrimental to teacher–pupil interactions. Some students felt that this was a form of stereotyping, and of racism. One student's account of just such an incident is an interesting example:

> Jesse: *We have an administrator who thinks that we all look alike. He calls all of us by the same name. I would love to see him smarten up. The other day I was walking past the office and he saw me and said that, "You don't go to the school." I said how did he know, and he said, "I know these things." He took me into the office, and he brought in Ms. Chalk, and said, "This student doesn't go to this school." She said, "Yes he does," and I said, "Thank you," and got up and left.*

The students complained that the teachers and their fellow students had a limited knowledge about countries that were populated by people of African descent. They indicated that the two main "countries" that fellow students associated with a Black population were Jamaica or "Africa":

> Lilieth: *They think we're all Jamaicans or African. Every Black person, that's it!*

> Pearl: *Like when you first meet them they think that you are from Jamaica . . . . They say yeah, Jamaica man* [said with fake Jamaican accent].

> Chorus: *I read that!*

> Grace: *They feel that they have to act different towards you . . . . This doesn't relate to school . . . me and my sister we both had braids . . . we went on a plane, the captain greets you, and he shakes hands with the passengers. And when we got on he says, "Yeah man!" I mean why does he have to say it to us?*

68

Yvonne: *I think it's what they see on TV.*

Grace: *They feel that they have to distinguish you from everyone else.*

Lilieth: *I was talking with this guy once and he goes to me, "Are you from Jamaica?" and I said "No," and he said "Africa," and I said "I am from Guyana," and he says, "Aren't Guyanese people White?"*

Yvonne: *No one knows where that is?*

Bev: *Even Trinidad, I've heard people say [where is it?].*

Yvonne: *That's what I found different from Toronto. There are a lot more Black people in Toronto, and they [Whites] know where these places are.*

Lack of knowledge about other ethnic groups as outlined above was not unidirectional and this resulted in Black students using the categorizations they accused others of using:

Grace: *It's the same, and of course you are going to get mad, but if I see a Chinese or Japanese whatever, because we have no way of knowing. [I won't be able to tell where they come from]. So of course . . . [we] are going to get mad but at the same time you can see why they [non-Blacks] automatically think you are from Jamaica.*

Some students felt that there were specific stereotypes that related to their academic potential. As one student stated:

George: *[We have to] show them that Black people are not drug dealers, pimps, hoes, not just sports people, "rappers" and singers. We are people that have high intelligence. They see us as someone who can do great "slam-dunks."*

Several students felt that even though the teachers did not express any open animosity or make direct negative verbal comments, they had to try extra hard to prove themselves in order to overcome the stereotype of Blacks as being non-academic.

Milton: *There are stereotypes in society. When Black people come to a class you can already feel that people think that a Black person is slack about classes, and that they'll skip and that they have been into all sorts of trouble . . . . Teachers have perceptions of Black people and Chinese people . . . . I'm sure if a Black person did the same work, that the Chinese person would automatically get a higher grade because they are Chinese and teachers expect them to be good. For Black people they [teachers] already have the assumption that they are not too bright, school is not their thing.[7]*

A prevalent stereotype in society is that Blacks have a natural ability to excel at sports. This construction, especially in relation to males, is one to which various studies have attested.[8] In a Toronto high school Patrick Solomon (1992; 1994) found a pervasive sports subculture among the Black males he interviewed. From the interviews and the questionnaires that some students filled out, it is obvious that they were aware of sports personalities, particularly male American sports personalities constructed by the media. For example, over the past decade there has been a growth in the popularity of basketball both as a sport to participate in and a sport to watch. Among those cited as being admired by the students in my research were Charles Barkley, Shaquille O'Neal and Michael Jordan,[9] all of whom are Black. The reasons given for admiring sports personalities tended to be that they were "ruff necks" and "spoke their minds" or were of "rough appearance and didn't care what others thought."

The females I interviewed also chose mostly American males as their favourite sports personalities. Flo-Joe, Florence Kearsy Joiner, the single female sports personality chosen, was liked because

Alice: *she's a strong role model . . . persistent, and won many medals in the Olympics; she doesn't let anything stand in her way.*

The predominance of males in female choices of sports persons admired is probably a reflection of the dominant exposure of Black male athletes as compared to Black female athletes in the visual media.[10] For the majority of students, sport stars are attractive not just because they excel at their chosen sport and are given media exposure, but also because of their personalities and how they interact with mainstream society. Perhaps this is what Michael Dyson is alluding to when he suggests that "Black sports heroes transcend the narrow boundaries of specific sports activities and garnered importance as icons of cultural excellence, symbolic figures who embodied social possibilities of success denied to other people of colour" (1993: 66).

The importance of sports to Black males was attested to by Desmond who, when discussing the effects of the education cuts applied by the Klein government in Alberta, suggested that:

> *If you cut down phys ed a lot of Black kids are going to stop coming to school 'cause they got a lot of basketball talent . . . want to play football . . . [and run] track.*

The stereotype of Blacks excelling at sports often becomes problematic when it falls prey to dualistic Western philosophy in which things are seen as "either/or." I would suggest that this stereotype tends to reinforce the idea that physical prowess is divorced from intellectual ability. Within the education system this duality can become a reality; for a student to excel at sports, he or she has to spend time honing physical skills, time which may well be needed for more academic pursuits. Also, as one student outlined, it is not always easy to tell a sports teacher that you would rather concentrate on your academic work than represent the school.

A teacher who supported the view that Blacks were associated with sports was asked:

> Jennifer: *Is there anything that Black students are noted for?*

> Ms. Eraser: *They get positives for being athletic but not for being good students.*

What we have is a position suggested to young Blacks, particularly males, that offers the possibility of success as shown by other Blacks who have followed this route. It also involves a strong emotional element that provides more fulfilment than the academic curriculum. It is interesting to note that although sports activities were popular among both males and females, the way it fits into their school lives was not the same for both genders.

> Desmond: *[With] women it's different, they are into the lawyer stuff—you never see a woman saying she wants to go into the NFL [National Football League].*

This gender difference in how sports was viewed as a future career may well be linked to the differing possibilities offered via media image to the different genders. Of those Black students who were involved in clubs or organizations related to the schools, the majority tended to be in sports related activities:

> Barrington: *A lot of us come together for track and field.*

Lack of time and interest were cited as reasons for not getting involved in other school-related activities. Very few were involved in student organizations such as the student council. It is therefore no surprise that for a few students, Black and non-Black, who found the academic stress at school alienating, sports was the main attraction of school.

> Delroy: *Valley High is a wicked school, me like the sports program . . . [me no need to learn other subjects 'cause] me can read and write and spell.*

Only a minority of students saw sports as a way to enhance their chances of getting scholarships. For others, the negative side of sports was that too heavy an involvement could compete with an academic career and thus allow them to fall into the trap of promoting the stereotype of the athletic Black male who does not excel academically.

Other stereotypes that the students mentioned related to Blacks being seen as "rough" and "bad."[11] Some students indicated that this meant that at times other students seemed to fear them, sometimes solving this fear by being over zealous in trying to become friends. It should be noted that this stereotype could also be "played up" and adopted by some of the Black students, especially males. The stereotype of being "bad," as with many stereotypes, can be seen as a dual construct. As well as engendering fear and causing others to keep their distance, it can also have the reverse effect and cause other groups to want to prove themselves physically, thus causing fights.

Style

Dress and style are also manifestations of the process of stereotyping (Hebdige 1979). The Black students' school lives illustrated how dress and style became part of their racial identity and affected how others reacted to them. *U.S. Today* noted in 1990 that there was a rising crossover appeal of Black fashion—twisted braids, dreadlocks, hi-top fades, L.A. Raiders gear, banana headbands, African beads, baggy clothes—which it called Afrocenchic (cited in George 1992:37).[12] The emergence of this style of dressing has been linked to the sneaker, and the increased popularity of basketball. Icons such as Black basketball player Michael Jordan epitomized the growth in popularity of the sport as well as the basketball sneaker. Michael Dyson notes how the sneaker is more than a shoe in the representation of a subcultural period: "[T]he sneaker reflects at once the projection and stylization of Black urban realities linked in our contemporary historical moment to rap culture and the underground political economy of crack and reigns as the universal icon of cultural consumption" (1993: 70).

The students were asked to describe what "dressing Black" entailed. The following interview is representative of their responses:

> Jennifer: *So what does "dressing Black" mean?*

> Joy: *Baggy pants, high top shoes, extensions, stuff like that. You mostly see them [non-Black students] in those bell foot pants. You just look and say that's Black.*

The description by the students is very reminiscent of the "Afrocenchic" style described by the *U.S. Today* report. What is interesting about the mesh of these two perspectives is that "dressing Black" seems to be a label that is ascribed to Black students rather than one that they consciously adopted. In other words, this component of their identity is received as well as given by the youths.

Some students challenged the idea that there was a uniform way of "dressing Black." These students suggested that many of them tended to apply their own stamp of individuality on a style of dressing that was common among their peers. For example, for a group of close male friends the head was often used as a site for expressing differences in style. One young man wore his hair in "circular cane rows," another in a beehive look, one had dyed his hair and another had tiny plaits. As Everton put it:

> *We all try to be different . . . . It may be the same haircut [but we do different things to it].*

In conjunction with hair, the group also used headgear as a means of asserting difference. Often, a hat was worn on top of the bandanna, adding considerable height to the head as well as circumventing the "no bandanna" rules applied in some malls. Some students used their head as a site of "bricolage," whereby the meaning of everyday objects is changed by putting them in a different context (Levi-Strauss 1966). A male student attested to meaning being attached to specific aspects of clothing when he commented that clothes such as the handkerchief are worn by "wiggers" ("White niggers") without them knowing their full significance and the historical context from which the pieces of clothing emerged.[13] This young man was part of a group that used their form of dress to indicate and declare their Blackness. The group members had an affinity with Jamaica and as such wore various colours associated with Jamaica and Rastafarians. Some members of this group indicated that their style was similar to the way that they themselves had dressed in Jamaica. For some members dress was seen at times as signification of Blackness and as a way of maintaining a collective memory of being Black. Bob, who was censured in this group, explains how dress was equated with Blackness:

> There's the style with all the colours. [Then] there's a whole bunch
> of guys that dress normally, or we call normal, just jeans and boots
> and T-shirts. And they [other Black males] say that we have lived
> here too long.

Other students challenged the idea that they dressed in any defined way
and explained that their tastes in dress were unconsciously acquired. For
example, Lester's choice was based on what he perceived suited him:

> I always wear black . . . you never catch me without something
> black . . . . If [I see someone] and they look good and I think it will
> look good, I'll get it.

However, we can suggest that since many tastes are often affected by
external influences in the form of media, peers and marketing strategies,
these choices of clothing are not "innocent." As Hebdige explains:

> [E]ach ensemble has its place in an internal system of differ-
> ences—the conventional modes of sartorial discourse—which
> form a corresponding set of socially prescribed roles and options.
> These choices contain a whole range of messages, which are
> transmitted through the finely graded distinctions of a number of
> interlocking sets—class status, self-image and attractiveness, etc.
> Ultimately, if nothing else they are an expression of "normality"
> as opposed to deviance (i.e., they are distinguished by their rela-
> tive invisibility, their appropriateness, their "naturalness"). (1979:
> 101)

Although in a minority on this issue, Everton admitted that he dressed
consciously in order to convey a meaning:

> Byron relates back to what he wore in Jamaica. I dress like O'Dog
> [a character in "Menace II Society"]. I like to look rough. The only
> time we dress good is when we go to reggae parties.

During a female focus group some of the young women indicated that
for them dressing in what many termed a Black style of baggy clothing
allowed them more freedom of movement. This style was considered more
practical for school; that they dressed very differently when they were
going to a reggae party or hall party. The "preppy style" favoured by some
White girls involved wearing the more constricting lacy blouses and

74

platform shoes. Class also played a role in dress as "preppy" girls saw the style of dress worn by some Black girls as a reflection of their low socio-economic status.

Several Black students and some teachers indicated that being Black was "cool." This may be attributable to the subcultural attraction of Black culture[14] "which rests on its evocation of an age-old image of blackness: a foreign sexually charged, criminal underworld against which the norms of White society are defined, and by extension, through which they may be defined" (Samuels, cited in Koza 1994: 191). These processes allow Whites to embrace the perceived "danger" of Black culture with the knowledge that they can return to White mainstream culture eventually (Hebdige 1979). The expression of this "coolness" seems to emanate from the dress and music associated with Black people. Videos that accompany most hip-hop music enhance the visual portrayal of cool images of Black people as well as of the youth culture that surrounds the alienated youths in the urban areas of the U.S. Julia Koza suggests that with the advent of videos and music recordings Whites can consume Black culture without face-to-face contact. She highlights that, although the media represents and aligns Black identity with "gangsta rap," in fact since 1990 a large percentage of this type of music has been consumed by White, often middle-class, youths. An article in *Esquire* (Carroll 1994) discusses the association of some Whites with perceived Black style and how other Whites come to perceive such adoption of "Black styles" as a symbolic threat to White mainstream American values.[15]

SUMMARY

Ranging from media sources such as music, film and television to church and family, the students have access to a wide variety of interpretations of Blackness that they can identify with or adopt in their formation of a Black identity. The descriptor Black is complex and multi-layered; the ways in which a textual source, for example, will be received or perceived by the students is unpredictable. Black identification is adapted by the students as they interact with the various sources available to Black youth in a White society. From the narratives we can see that Black identity is both ascribed and achieved. In terms of style and music there is evidence to support Paul Gilroy's (1993) postulation that we need to reconceive Black culture in terms of an Atlantic diaspora developed from movement between America, Europe, the Caribbean and Africa. Further, those students who have knowledge of the social and economic position of Blacks in other White-dominated societies demonstrated a sense of collective memory.

The ability of a source to "lure" or "call" students varied according to their age, class, gender and the amount of influence that their family had, and was not final or forever. Thus for a student to be able to identify with a film character such as O' Dogg, he or she would have to be able to find the time and space within his or her life to adopt constituents of such an identification. "Black style" can be seen as an innocent aspect of youth culture, or as a more provocative tool of posturing and intimidation. How the style is viewed and received is based on the attitude and gait that goes along with the clothes, as illustrated in Chapter One during my discussion of being under the gaze and glaring.

NOTES

1. "Collective memory" indicates the degree of knowledge about the position of Blacks in White-dominated societies. Some students used it as a form of resistance to social control. As Homi K. Bhabha has suggested, the obligation to forget in the name of unity is a form of "violence involved in establishing the national writ" (1990: 310).

2. "Crossover" is a term used in cultural studies literature to describe an art form's movement in popularity across racial and social-class groups. Janet Peck (1994) analyzes how the Oprah Winfrey show constructed the issue of "race" during a series of shows.

3. Discussion of how the news projects the actions of individuals onto a specific social group is illustrated by Duart Farquharson's article in the *Edmonton Journal,* June 26, 1994. Farquharson responded to criticism of the resident cartoonist who drew a cartoon that linked the misdemeanor of individual Blacks to Blacks as a social group.

4. "Boundary maintenance" refers to the ability of social groups to use aspects of everyday social interaction to maintain a separation between groups, in this case between Blacks and non-Blacks.

5. Though it is complex to define, I refer to "racism" as "the doctrine that unjustifiably asserts the superiority of one group over another on the basis of arbitrarily selected characteristics pertaining to appearance, intelligence or temperament" (Elliott and Fleras 1992: 52). Much discussion has been going on recently about whether Blacks can be racist towards Whites. I have decided to adopt an understanding whereby prejudice and bigotry can be displayed by all ethnic groups towards each other, but the term racism is more precisely applied when a relation of economic and social dominance also exists between two ethnic groups. To be racist an individual has to belong to an ethnic or raced group that has the ability to affect the life chances of the other group to participate fully within specific areas of society. Intent does not have to be present; with racism consequences are important (Sarup 1991). Recent theorizing around issues of power related to Foucault renders this definition problematic. For Foucault, power is not an either/or concept. This means that he would be unlikely to subscribe to a theoretical position that sees racism as one-dimensional, always imposed from above.

6. Collins (1990) makes a similar point in her analysis of the role that Black women have undertaken as educators with a responsibility for "racial uplift" within the wider community and in African American churches. Refer also to

the *Edmonton Bulletin's* "Our Negro Citizen" column January 28, 1922.

7. This comment is important if one bears in mind the concept of a self-fulfilling prophecy. This latter theory illustrates the way in which teacher expectation results in differing educational outcomes for students. Expectations are often based upon ascribed characteristics such as sex and physical appearances, or characteristics that students take on as a result of their achievements, aspirations or attitudes (Rosenthal and Jacobson 1968; Rist 1970).

8. Stereotypes based on sports are prevalent in literature in Britain and North America.

9. These interviews were conducted before the increased media attention given to Dennis Rodman and Donovan Bailey.

10. The journal *Women and Physical Sports* outlines how sports women are constructed as "Other" in relation to men.

11. The construction of Blacks as "rough" and "bad" can be seen in the televisual aspects discussed earlier in this chapter, and also in the discussion of style that follows. See Peter McLaren's "Multiculturalism and the Postmodern Critique" (1993: 119–20) for his comments on the White-dominated media's construction of Blacks as violent.

12. This terminology is problematic since it is debatable whether a whole community can be typified as adopting this style, and doubtful that the style can be traced directly to Africa.

13. It is important to note the way that Desmond uses the idea of collective memory to reinforce the present. Although he berates the "wiggers" for not knowing the historical roots of the wearing of the handkerchief (as dating back to slavery), one wonders how many of the Black youth that wear the handkerchief know its historical origins. "Wiggers" is the term used for Whites who associate themselves with aspects of perceived Black culture or Blacks as a social group. Some female students were so labelled in River High, where there was indication that some White students also used the term derogatively. For some Black students "wiggers" were symbolic of White appropriation.

14. hooks (1992) and Dick Hebdige make a similar point, concerning "the search for adventure and excitement . . . which coexist with and undercut the sober positives of mainstream society (routinization, security, etc.)" (Hebdige 1979: 44).

15. The article outlines how so called "wiggers" have been ostracized by White students because of the way they dress. For these White students, the form of dress is recognizably Black and therefore reflective of the "Other." As one of these so called "wigger" students states in the article: "Some guys started saying that we're trying to dress Black and everything . . . . And they started calling us 'wiggers,' and at first they were just writing stuff on desks like 'Wiggers,' and 'White Power' and 'KKK' and a bunch of stuff . . . . And then they started shoving us and they started spitting on us" (Carroll 1994: 103).

CHAPTER FOUR

Relating to Peers

Milton: *[When you're] with Whites you are always Black, they refer to your Blackness . . . with other Blacks you are just another person.*

The students' view of themselves and the knowledge they have of what it means to be Black affects their relationships with other raced groups. This chapter highlights the way in which the students' perceptions of themselves as Black are mediated in their relations with other ethnic groups. Again, "knowing where you're coming from," linked to the theme of "collective memory," affects the degree and depth of social interaction that takes place between Black youths and their non-Black peers. In looking at how Black students interact with others in school and beyond we see that, although experiences vary, there are commonalities based on assumptions and perceptions of "racial" identity. My interviews illustrate the phenomenon of racialization.

Clustering: Organizational Aspects

The number of Black students in an institution affects the degree of interaction between Black students and students of other ethnic groups. The students described how their high school experiences differed from those at the junior high level. For many, high school offered the first opportunity to mix with Blacks who were not members of their church or from their immediate neighbourhood.

Elementary and junior high schools, which had few Black students, provided the opportunity for some students to mix socially with a variety of raced groups.

Barrington: *There was not that many Black people in my elementary school so I had to get along with other people. In junior high there was still a little bit more [Black students] but not that many. But it was in high school in grade 10 that you associate more [with Blacks].*

The racial isolation of elementary and junior high meant that Black students experienced an early school career peppered by racial slurs and insults.[1]

> George: *It starts in elementary; that's where usually every person has heard the name "nigger" and you hear it so much . . . . Nobody really does much . . . 'cause you're just a kid.*

Youths recalled how, in elementary and junior high, racial taunts resulted in Black students getting into fights. When this occurred Black students often perceived themselves as receiving more severe disciplinary consequences than the perpetrator of the fight. Many felt the disciplinary decisions were unfair; for them physical action was a justifiable response to racial taunting:

> Zora: *My brother is always getting into fights over that [the word nigger]. . . . Always my dad has to go down to the school.*

> Bev: *I think that every Black person who has been in elementary, that's the word they grew up with.*

> Grace: *My sister is in grade 8 and someone called her a "nigger" or a porch monkey or something, and my sister punched her, and my sister got suspended and I don't think she should get suspended for that . . . . That's verbal abuse, it's the same as physical abuse . . . . Are you teaching her she can't stick up for herself?*

Students suggest that some parents shared their perspectives on how to deal with racial taunting:

> Lorraine: *At junior high I was getting into fights . . . 'cause of people calling me nigger . . . . [You] go to the teacher and they don't do a thing . . . . When you hit them [the perpetrators] back you get into trouble . . . . My mum went to the principal and told him that she was the one who had told me to hit these people back.*

The latter reveals a miscommunication between teachers and parents, which has important ramifications for interactions between students and teachers. If parents tell their children that they should "stand up" for themselves when taunted and teachers view this type of reaction as inappropriate, then we have a clash of perspectives that can be detrimental to Black students.[2]

Students described how overt name calling lessened in high school. However, they associated this decrease with the greater presence of Black students and the recognition by non-Black students that if they persisted with taunts such as "nigger" there would be physical consequences.

> Phyllis: *In junior high and elementary, because the population of Black people is very low, the White kids tend to tease you a lot more . . . because your hair is different or something else. But I notice once you get into high school the White kids won't say anything to you; they give you more respect, probably because they're afraid.*

The youths suggested that the absence of overt racist comments does not mean that the student population is more tolerant. Rather, their comments indicate a greater racial sophistication on the part of non-Black students; they are able to ascertain when it is socially acceptable and less physically threatening to use racial slurs. This speculation was supported by Black youths who said they saw racism as being present, but hidden.[3] Youths highlighted the differing ways in which racialization takes place in the U.S. and Canada.

> George: *In New York, and L.A. they'll say, "Get the fuck away from me I don't like you." . . . But here . . . they'll say it behind your back.*

> Toni: *In the States, if you are Black they'll say so. I think that's better—'cause they [White Canadians] are smiling in your face and stabbing you in your back at the same time.*

> Lorraine: *This multiculturalism thing they have in Canada is a complete joke. They [Whites] don't believe in that!*

Some Black youths found this subtle functioning of racialization potentially more damaging than overt racial hostility because it could lead to a situation where they presumed a higher level of acceptance than existed.

Just as the number of Black students in a school affects raced interaction, so does the number of Black students in the classroom affect interactions. Alice and Barrington described how in their classrooms students mixed freely with other raced groups:

> Alice: *In all my classes there are not a lot of Blacks . . . so I am not just going to sit in my class and be all miserable [and say], "Oh you are not Black."*

> Barrington: *In my class it's mostly Whites so you have to talk to them, and as long as they don't act rude to me and they don't think that they are better than me then I talk to them.*

Even though there was a greater degree of mixing in his classroom, Milton indicated that the level of conversation between students was superficial and related to school.

> *We talk about teachers and schools . . . the stuff you talk about is limiting.*

Teachers in the high schools under discussion also commented on the difference between interactions within formalized groupings such as classes and other forms of groupings that were student-initiated.

> Jennifer: *Is there much clustering?*

> Ms. Eraser: *A lot of that in the last few years. Lebanese, Black groups, Chinese, there is not a lot of mixture. The classes I have got are fairly integrated . . . although if they can they like to cluster. Like the Chinese would like to talk Chinese. The Lebanese would like to sit with each other. I try to move them around.*

> Ms. Looseleaf: *They tend to stick together in little cliques. If you go to the cafeteria at noon, it's mostly Oriental kids . . . and the area around my classroom. A lot of the Black kids tend to stick together, part of that is that they formed a "step" team,[4] so that's group cohesive there . . . . It really depends what their interests are. A lot of the school council kids tend to be A.P. [advanced placement] students.[5]*

Milton's analysis revealed how some of this fragmentation occurs:

> *This high school is big, you have to talk to people that have something in common with you, interested in the things you are interested in. There are different White groups . . . hippy White people, headbanger White people. Blacks have circles of friends . . . you know pretty much every Black person.*

Thus the size of the high school as well as the number of Black students affects social interaction. Large organizations tend to fragment as the individuals within them attempt to find meaning in their situation. One of the common points of interest and experiences for these youths was the way in which their peers perceived and reacted to them as Other.

Friends

Outside of the classroom, within the corridors and confines of the school where organizational constraints are not present, students have a greater degree of say over with whom they interact. Friends are "significant others" for all youths at this stage of development. Both male and female students interviewed identified common traits that they sought in a friend. Trust and having the time to listen and show concern emerged as strong necessities for long-term friendships. In spite of the fact that all raced groups possess these attributes, the Black youths interviewed chose their close friends mainly, though not exclusively, from the Black student population. Such friends were often seen as having a perceived closer tie than non-Black students. Students described this closer tie as the ability to "act natural." Acting natural involved feeling relaxed and not being on guard when socially interacting with others. Milton described this comfort level as being more achievable when interacting with fellow Blacks.

> [When you're] with Whites you are always Black, they refer to your Blackness . . . with other Blacks you are just another person.

A few students indicated that they had maintained close non-Black friends from their earlier school years. These friendships tended to be maintained on the basis of the students' common experiences and support for each other through difficult times.

> George: I have one friend from then [junior high], he understands me to the fullest and he's a White guy. He doesn't act Black, he doesn't really listen much to Black music, he's into "grunge" music.

> Malcolm: What's kept you together all these years?

> George: Little kids hanging out together, having snowball fights, doing little kids things, being there for me when I was getting busted for doing this and that. I was there for him. We went skateboarding together. We just did things as little kids and as you grow up you begin to have respect for those things. It's easier to be friends with somebody at that age than it is now. At our age everything is about money and it's a different aspect.

Non-Black individuals in a cross-racial friendship must also be willing to allow space for a Black friend to mix with other Black students.

Ida: *We've come through rough times . . . she knows I have Black friends. We respect each other's space. She'll throw a birthday party for me and I'll throw one for her.*

Alice pointed out, though, that when non-Black friends see Blacks as a separate negative group it can have consequences for the friendship:

Alice: *A lot of my White friends who I went to junior high with say I'm different. [They say,] "You've changed, you are like all the rest, ever since you've been hanging around with them!"*

Even though cross-racial friendships exist, the Black youths indicated that they could not assume that racism had been eradicated from their relationships. Because someone has a Black friend does not mean that they are free of racism and are affable towards other Black youths. As Toni suggested:

[Whites say] my best friend is Black . . . well you can have a Black friend and you can still see them as under you.

"Hanging out" socially is often a complex experience reflecting gendered and raced identities. For a few students this experience involved mixing extensively with other raced groups.

Jennifer: *Do you mix with any other groups socially?*

Lynford: *Yeah, Orientals, with some of the White guys . . . they take me to this place called [Pinball]. We go out to parties. When we go out to parties it's like . . . a mixed culture, White guys, Black guys, Orientals and so on . . . . And there will be a whole bunch of guys walking . . . . Sometimes it seems unusual, but it's not really 'cause that's the way things are going to turn out hopefully.*

Social interaction outside the confines of school reinforced some of the raced/ethnic boundaries found in the schools. For example, some of the churches attended by the students have a predominantly Black congregation, and consequently some of the students continued to mix with fellow Black students from school. This mixing also affected in-school friendship patterns, especially for church-going female students such as Ida:

I have friends who go to my church, people who I know before . . . . We stick to our own [church] cliques; we don't do a lot of things that they [non-church students] do . . . . We don't go to reggae dances, but we will still talk . . . . As a church group, we've grown up, we have rules and regulations and some things that we can't talk about . . . . So in order for me not to be tempted I keep away [from non-church cliques].

So we find that paradoxically, while the church assists in the maintenance of raced solidarity by offering alternative identities, it is also implicated in differentiating between Blacks, as the type of "moral" identity it offers is not acceptable to all.

Hall parties[6] and reggae dances were popular places for the students to socialize. These activities have a predominantly Black following, which increases its attractiveness to Black youths as a place where they can feel more comfortable and "act natural"; people will "know where you are coming from" as they feel those with whom they are socializing have something in common. Alice outlined how this common tie could change and affect high school friendship patterns:

Jennifer: *Do you socialize [with non-Blacks] outside of school?*

Alice: *Not much. People from my junior high I used to, but [now it's] mainly at school . . . . We don't go out of our way to do anything. I guess we've grown apart since junior high. Now I go out more to hall parties. The people I socialized with in junior high are different kind of people . . . . Even I'm a totally different person. It just wouldn't seem right [for them to attend hall parties]. They wouldn't fit.*

Jennifer: *Is that because they are a different group, or because of their personalities?*

Alice: *They don't like that kind of music.*

Jennifer: *Your musical tastes have changed?*

Alice: *Well, not changed. I was into more wide a variety of music. Well now, the things I listened to before I can't stand now.*

Jennifer: *Give me an example of what you used to listen to?*

Alice: *I used to listen to some alternative . . . it's what my friends were into . . . . Now I listen to mostly soul, R&B, '70s stuff and rap, reggae . . . . I listened to all that stuff before, it's just that I've sort of like narrowed it down.*

Many youths indicated that they would not consider taking non-Blacks to hall parties because non-Blacks might feel uncomfortable and would not know how to act. For some, like Jimmy, doing so would put him "under the gaze":

> Jennifer: *Would you take [a White person] to a reggae party?*

> Jimmy: *Most of them don't want to go 'cause they feel uncomfortable. 'Cause it's mostly Blacks . . . . I wouldn't go to an all White party. No, it's the same thing . . . 'cause you feel left out . . . . Different culture and they act different.*

> Jennifer: *Tell me how they act?*

> Jimmy: *They act different, they drink and they act crazy. At a reggae party, if you drink, you go in a corner by yourself . . . . They like making mother jokes, well I don't like that 'cause I respect my mom.*

Jimmy's reference to drink reflects comments by other youths interviewed that alcohol plays a bigger role in the social lives of young Whites. Many of these narratives suggested that for White youths having fun means going to bush parties, boasting about weekend drinking sprees involving "throwing up," and generally being "out of control."

Although the characteristics of a friend were not specific to one raced group, most of the youths interviewed described how they chose to spend their leisure time with friends from their own raced/ethnic group. This choice was partly based on aspects of youth culture, such as music, and someone understanding "where you're coming from." Most rationalized this choice in terms of "feeling comfortable"—as discussed in Chapter One, they were no longer under the gaze.

Hanging Together

The degree of inter-racial interaction among students can be placed on a continuum whereby some Black students mix with one or two non-Black students, while others tend to "move" in larger Black groups. At the other end of the continuum is the greatest level of Black solidarity: groups of males form self-designated "crews." A crew is a "clique" or group of friends who "hang together" and "move together," both in and out of school. This type of group of close friends who were interviewed during this project was able to spend more time together than most because they had access to their own accommodation, were not under the close supervision of their parents.

> Jennifer: *What would you call a good friend?*

> Lester: *We are always together . . . twenty-four hours day and night. In between classes, lunch, after school at my place . . . . In school we hang out in the cafeteria.*

In addition to the time spent together in and out of school, music reinforced links within the crews. Members of both of the friendship crews interviewed followed a reggae sound system and had members with connections to Jamaica. Many of the crew members were born there; some had visited for a period of time or had connections through their parents.

> Melvin: *I lived in the States for a while . . . . [I] left when I was four years old and moved to Jamaica. When I was six or seven, I moved here.*

The crew members' cultural backgrounds are important to maintaining their group solidarity. Often the students' conversations were related to places in Jamaica, things that happened in a certain parish, or how their parents raised them. They could relate to the ways of behaving and interacting that they recognized as having developed from the social structures of the Caribbean. They considered that they "knew where each other were coming from."

> Everton: *All of us are Jamaican background. It's like we are all the same. I'll say something like, "When I was young my mom used to hit me and go why are you crying" . . . and they'll say, "Yeah! yeah! [our] mom used to say that."*

Crew cohesiveness is also reinforced by the members' present school interactions. Desmond and Malcolm spoke of these school interactions:

> Desmond: *We need a population. And [when we are in a minority] it's better we come together; then if one person tries to put us down we have the crew behind us. That's one of the main reasons I came here [because of the large numbers of Blacks].*

> Jennifer: *So why do you "hang out" together?*

> Desmond: *It's more educational. At least when we are together, we talk about ourselves more, than if you are with a White group. You*

might learn more about yourself when you hang out with your own.

Malcolm: *Most of the time when we sit in the cafe, he might come from Jamaica, I come from Trinidad and he might be from St Lucia. Then we talk about each other's islands. It's good to bring back a little bit of the home.*

These comments illustrate how the strength of raced bonds is maintained because they serve a purpose. Students are maintaining a link with knowledge of their past, they are getting affective feedback from discussing familiar aspects of their socialization process.

There is also an element of protection in being with a group rather than being an isolated individual. Desmond highlighted how raced groups could be particularly advantageous at specific times:

We met each other in the mall. We were sitting and talking about all the Black people that come together. That was the time we were having the school problem with Lebanese . . . . A lot of Black guys were getting beaten up by Lebanese. So we said this is what we have to do. That's how I met Eldridge and Byron.

Jennifer: *What things does your group represent?*

Desmond: *It's not that they have to have anything to join our group . . . . If you have a Black guy out there who is by himself . . . as they say a "geek" or a "nerd." We'll bring him in and let him know what's up and how to bring himself around. It's not that we have a group and we are going out to recruit. It's just there. A kid who doesn't hang around . . . who doesn't look like he has any friends. If we see a Black guy being beaten up by other groups or whatever then we also sometimes get involved in that too.*

The two friendship crews, although maintaining a strong Black male base, did not seem to overtly discourage their associates from mixing with other raced groups. However, some friendship groups did, in fact, actively refrain from mixing socially with non-Blacks.

Lynford: *We have one leader, and he says if you have a friend go talk to them. Don't be held back by what those [other Black] guys say.*

Jennifer: *Do you find that as a young Black man you relate just to other young Black men or do you have friends from other groups?*

Lester: *See that's what makes us different too [to some groups of Black males] . . . . These guys think they can go around beating up White people and just be friends with Black people when really that's how you start to make the two different. We go around we talk to anyone. Doesn't matter who you are, what colour you are, as long as you are allright. I talk to you as long as you talk to me . . . . I hate no one.*

Fights and Disputes

The two friendship crews studied had a "rough" image because they were perceived as able to handle themselves. They emphasized that they did not see themselves as predatory, but rather they reacted to aggression.

Everton: *I don't pick fights, but if anyone comes to me I'll fight them.*

The crews often referred to the protective social behaviours within their groups. As Lester said:

My boys will always back me. We protect each other like brothers. No one can come and do anything to one of us and get away. If some one messes with one of us, then they are "messin'" with all of us.

Everton: *We stick up for one another . . . . If somebody try to put one of them down, we'll come back and cut you down.*

For all the youths trust was an essential ingredient of friendship, but for the crews it was crucial. Eldridge, a member of the crew that seemed to interact more frequently with the police, indicated:

Some people talk too much, they'll sell you out. We stick to people we can trust.

Similarly Everton revealed:

I know [my friends] are not going to let me down; they are not going to sell out on me. Things have happened and they have not.

This group loyalty was often a factor in escalating disputes between the friendship crews and other groups and individuals mainly outside of school. For Everton's crew, although they fought primarily Chinese or Vietnamese youth, the initial cause of the dispute was not always overtly racial. As Desmond explained when describing a feud with an ethnic group that spilled over into school:

> It's not school violence . . . it's something that happen with Byron and a girl . . . . The girl was dealing with this Vietnamese guy [he was her boyfriend], he gave her money, and she came back and spent it on Byron. [The Vietnamese guy] found out and told his friends and they were trying to beat up Byron . . . . And Byron is with us, and we are ready to defend him. So all this violence started.

In both River High and Valley High the students described the level of school-based violence between raced groups as low. However, individual males had disputes, based on girls or derogatory comments, which then escalated into disputes involving not only those individuals but also their friends. Group loyalty is high among all youths, Black and non-Black, at this stage of social development. When group loyalty and ethnic cohesion come together they give disputes a racial edge. Although described by a number of students as not overtly racial, many of the disputes exhibited signs of racialization.

Students in both schools commented on the nature of the violence. They indicated that often disputes seemed to linger as each side would retaliate. Disputes were unlikely to be settled by a solitary fight. At Valley High the process worked in this way:

> Grace: Everyone wants to be the roughest group, and as soon as anyone challenges that or tests that, then they have to prove themselves, it doesn't end . . . . Before, in junior high if someone fought with another [student] and you beat them up, fine. It's done. Now, if I was to beat her up, she'll come and get her sister after me. Then I'll come and get my uncle after her . . . and it doesn't end.

> Lilieth: Someone has to come out on top.

> Hazel: If you lose you have to come back and make sure that you win.

> Grace: People never let a thing die, three years later, they will still be talking about it.

Many of the fights described involved males, but fights have occurred between females. The students suggested that often females would fight over young men, or over gossip and "hear say." As with young men "name calling" was also a trigger for retaliation. Ada recalled one incident:

> *A Chinese girl called [someone] "nigger" and [the Black girl] called her a "nip" . . . . All the girls went looking for the girl . . . and the Chinese girl got her relatives . . . . There was almost a big fight.*

For one of the friendship crews, fights were mainly part of their out-of-school lives. However, often this part of their lives had a strong impact on their social interaction within school. For example, two students who had been involved in fights with groups outside of school were no longer attending school, having gone "underground" according to the administrators. The majority of fights that took place away from school were with non-White groups, a factor that reflects the multicultural nature of their environment and also relates to issues of power as groups fight for status and prestige. Fights with Whites were not as frequent. Further, fighting was not more common among the general population of Black males than among other raced male groups. At the time of the study, fighting was specific to Eldridge's group. There was a crossover of friendship patterns between the two schools studied as some students had moved from River High to Valley High the previous year. The staff at both schools recognized that the students had outside school lives, but felt that their area of responsibility, as teachers, related primarily to those aspects of the students' behaviour that were displayed at school.

Mr. Ink, an administrator, believed most Black students found school to be a positive experience; the young Black males experiencing difficulties were seen as an insignificant minority:

> *Problems that do arise . . . [involve] the fringe who are not happy with their lot, not particularly with their family situation. They don't like coming to school and they like to get into mischief.*

Just as there are emotional and social advantages to being part of a friendship crew, there are also disadvantages. Close knit groups sometimes gain negative recognition as they come under the gaze of school administrators and the police. In observing the lifestyle of some of these young men who moved in a friendship crew I saw the reproduction of the stereotype and construction of young Black men as aggressive criminals. Members of this male friendship group were developing criminal records, alongside their poor academic records, which did not bode well for their post high school careers.

STEPPING OUT

For many of the young women in both schools studied, the step team was the basis of their friendships, and their primary type of involvement in extra curricular activities. Stepping has been popularized in the U.S. and is equated with a Black identity:

> Alice: *Next year, it's going to be lots of White people want to join it. It's a shame 'cause now it's a Black thing.*

> Grace: *The way I feel sometimes it's like White people do every-thing we do . . . . Sometimes I want to keep things just to Black people.*

Although males are involved in activities such as coaching and selecting music, stepping is regarded primarily as a female activity. At the school it served a dual purpose by being the focus for a Black activity, as well as reinforcing a sense of cohesiveness among many of the Black young women.

> Lorraine: *[Step] is important to a lot of us . . . . It's where we can be in a group without being hassled.*

Gender cohesiveness based on stepping was fragmented by constructions based on religion. For example, young women who were deeply involved with evangelical churches had ethical objections to music being used for dancing. Their main point of objection was that dancing to music for non-religious purposes contradicted the values espoused in their church com-munity. It should also be noted that for some of these young women, religious or not, step dance was not an activity in which they chose to participate.

Stepping was also seen by many students as a reason to attend school, especially when compared to the more static aspects of the formal curriculum. Stepping offers many of the elements that students would like to see in schoolwork. It enables students to work together, it is related to Black experience, it is active and students have a voice in its construction and development.

Although there was a sense among the students of group cohesiveness based on the experience of being Black women in a predominantly White society, interactions were not always smooth. At times individual experiences and personalities cut across this cohesiveness, with the result that at varying times a degree of tension emerged within the groups:

Lorraine: *The step team is good . . . you have your fights but basically everyone is friends.*

Jennifer: *What do you fight about?*

Lorraine: *When it gets to crunch time, the pressure, we get on each others' nerves . . . certain things people do set you off. You think "no fooling around this is the real thing" and everyone is fooling around. It just drives you up the wall. Then other people will decide to have a bit of fun to ease the tension, [and] other people want to start working.*

Mr. Pencil, a teacher, attested to this periodic tension among the young women and indicated that often they were very vocal when an individual got "out of line":

Girls get very upset with each other. When they get upset, boy, do you know it. I talk to some and they say they all take care of each other. If one of them does something stupid they let them know.

Both Black males and females within the two schools regarded the team with pride. Teachers also indicated that the teams were regarded highly by the staff and non-Black pupils within the schools.

Ms. Looseleaf: *The step team gets a lot of respect in our school, most of the kids prefer the step team to the cheerleaders.*

Mr. Pencil: *I like the concept and the team. Every slide show we make a point of having the step team. We get them to perform whenever we can . . . . They are responsible and dedicated.*

In River High the team was not officially recognized as a school team, mainly as a result of the team's tardiness in registering with the school's council. This lack of official status caused various problems for the team. Some members perceived these negative experiences—not being officially recognized as a school team and lacking financial support to buy outfits—as the result of a lack of support and a tinge of racism on the part of the school administration.

Bessie: *The school doesn't support us at all . . . not like the cheerleaders who get their own outfits . . . their socks even.*

The students' perceptions are interesting in light of the teachers' indications that the school esteemed the step team. The teachers made the liberal assumption that as long as they treated everyone exactly the same way, regardless of circumstances, and followed the rules, they were being "fair" and equality was achieved. For the students, treating everyone the same way regardless of the circumstances did not lead to an equal outcome. As well as comparing their treatment with other sports groups within their school, the team compared their situation to that of another school's step team, which seemed to have administrative support as well as verbal recognition for their efforts. The students saw their treatment as resulting from their being Black and the consequent stereotypes on which teachers drew. One student suggested that the school did not respect a Black project, or the amount of time spent preparing for performances. The school was willing to "show them off" when it was convenient to do so, but not to give them official recognition. This highlighted a misperception between the two groups, and created a dilemma for the teachers who felt that they should not make any extra effort to help the team.

Patois

For some students whose families originated in the Caribbean, the issue of being able to "act natural" was sometimes linked to the use of language. Maintaining one's daily speech pattern is important:

> To deny ourselves daily use of speech patterns that are common and familiar, that embody the unique and distinctive aspect of ourselves is one of the ways we become estranged and alienated from our past. It is important for us to have as many languages on hand as we can know or learn. It is important for those of us who are Black, who speak in particular Patois as well as standard English to express ourselves in both ways. (hooks 1989: 79)

The students with close familial ties with Jamaica described how patois was used to varying degrees among themselves. Most, although not all, were able to switch from standard English to patois depending on to whom they were speaking. As Everton indicated when observing Desmond having a conversation with me:

> *I didn't know he could talk like that [standard English].*
> Bev: *We can all put on and off our Jamaican accents.*

In both schools many of the Black students with a Caribbean background could speak or understand patois, having acquired it from home and friends. However, many chose not to speak it in the classroom, preferring to keep it for use at home and between friends. Juliet indicated her choice of usage:

> *When I am in the classroom I speak English. Then when [other students] hear me round my Black friends talking patois, they're like, "How come you change your accent, how can you do that!" They think you are pretending. They think that if you're talking English in the classroom that's the way I talk all the time.*

Juliet's reluctance to use patois in the classroom may be due to the social stigma once associated with patois as a result of Jamaicans of high socio-economic status wrongly categorizing it as a form of "bad English." On the other hand, in Valley High males publicly used patois when they were annoyed with a teacher or wanted a "closed form of communication" between them:

> Jennifer: *Patois, you indicated that some people [mainly boys] used it. Could you explain that a bit further and give an example?*
>
> Maya: *If a teacher kicks them out of class they'll cuss.*
>
> Lilieth: *Say something so that the teacher can't understand them.*
>
> Maya: *The guys are like that.*
>
> Jennifer: *Is it something that they use as a group?*
>
> Pearl: *Sometimes when they are talking to each other when they get together.*
>
> Grace: *And when they get mad.*
>
> Lilieth: *Or trying to confuse their girlfriends* [laughter—because girlfriend's origins were North American not Caribbean].

For some of the male students who liked to use patois to "cuss," having a Black teacher who understood patois was a disadvantage as he or she was able to understand what was being said. This diluted the ability of patois to act as a form of closed communication. The following illustrates this situation:

> Jennifer: *How do the teachers react when the boys speak patois?*
>
> Lilieth: *Mr. Board reacts, the others don't. He is the only one that*

can understand it.

Pearl: *Some of the other teachers stand there and stare, what can they say, they can't understand it . . . . At [Parents Evening], Desmond and Ms. Chalk [a teacher] and all those boys were talking, and Ms. Chalk kept saying "What?" "What?" so in the end I had to tell her what they were saying.*

Lilieth: *Some of the boys were talking about that and they said that it wasn't fair because Mr. Board was getting on them, and if the Lebanese were swearing in their language, or the Chinese, he wouldn't know.*

Perceptions of Cohesion among Blacks and Other Racialized and Ethnic Groups in School

Although there was a great deal of cohesiveness among Black students, students at River High mentioned that there were sometimes splits within the Black group. For example, those who saw themselves as Jamaican and those who regarded themselves as Continental Africans at times distinguished themselves. Although the students did not articulate in detail why this was so, their narratives illustrated that raced groups can, at times, fragment into ethnic groups.

Everton: *The Africans don't like the Jamaicans and the Jamaicans don't like the Africans . . . . Any part of Africa, they all stay together, Somalia, Ghana. The only time they came together with us was on the soccer team.*

Ida: *A Black person called an African a jungle monkey and it caused trouble.*

Melvin: *I started hanging out with Africans [when I first came to school] then they talk about being Muslim, and [started saying] you Jamaicans this and that . . . . These [Jamaicans] guys is easier to relate to.*

Unity among Blacks in and out of the school environment was an issue for some students in River High. Varying perspectives were held. In relation to the school context some lamented that other students did not necessarily see that, in order to bring about changes beneficial to Blacks as a group, they would have to act as a "group for itself" not just as a "group in itself." In other words, Blacks have to be able to recognize their potential as a group, and use this to further their socio-economic status.

Using the Chinese and the Japanese as models, some of the students indicated that they would like to open up businesses that would employ mainly Blacks; they felt that at present the talents of young Blacks were underutilized in the mainstream economy. It was felt that for Blacks to progress as a group unity was necessary, but that in school life and in wider society Black students and Black adults in general did not seem willing to make a concerted effort to support Black-initiated projects.

> Milton: *Look at the Japanese people, they busted their butt . . . . They united as a country and set out some goals . . . and now they come here they've beaten the Whites at their own game . . . . They own their companies.*

> Bryan: *The Chinese are a good example of what Black people have to do. The only reason the Chinese succeed as well as they do is because they strive . . . . In order to be up there and not under the White man's power they have to succeed. They have suffered as well . . . . They help one another, they bring each other up in business and I think that's what Black people have to do.*

Interviews at both schools revealed that the students were not just aware of the treatment of their own raced group, but also of how other raced groups were treated and perceived at school. A few Black students mentioned First Nations students as being comparable to themselves in having encountered racism from White society. Lorraine and Toni saw this racism, even though their response was couched in stereotypical terms, as having a past that affected the present:

> Lorraine: *[The class] had a big discussion about Native Indians. I got into so many arguments with people. Even though they are not Black people I can understand where Natives are coming from. [The Whites] come onto their land and take everything and say to them, you can have this you can have that . . . and this is their own land!*

> Toni: *Yeah, you [First Nations people] can move up north where it well cold.*

> Lorraine: *I can feel for them . . . and them [Whites] blaming them 'cause they're drunk. Who gave them alcohol in the first place?*

> Toni: *Why is the reason they get drunk? Because they are trying*

to forget.

Jimmy indicated how his perception of the position of First Nations people in society had changed his behaviour:

> *I did it before, call them "chugs" [but not anymore]. There is always discrimination against Natives. They are looked down upon worse than Blacks in Canada.*

Comparisons between the experiences of some First Nations students and Blacks can be made both inside and outside the school. Ms. Eraser, a teacher, observed links between the schooling experiences of First Nations students and Black students:

> *I try to avoid [derogatory] things about Native Indians . . . that's another group that doesn't do well around this school. But the Blacks are following their trail . . . that's my perception.*

The students viewed other "visible" raced groups as also sticking together, and spoke of "the Chinese" and "the Lebs" in stereotypical terms. The teachers attested to this and to some of the implications:

> Jennifer: *Are there any conflicts that arise from these ethnic groupings?*

> Mr. Elastic: *Up until this year I would have said no, but I've been learning about events . . . [at a conference]. I listened to the kids talk about some of the ethnic difficulties in this school and I was surprised.*

> Jennifer: *Such as?*

> Mr. Elastic: *. . . fights between Chinese, Blacks, Lebanese, which I didn't know existed before.*

In keeping with stereotypical notions of a model minority, Chinese students were mentioned by some Black students, especially males, as being seen positively by the teachers as academic students, in contrast to the stereotype of the Black student. The Black students did not seem to have many close friends from the Chinese groups. Lebanese students had been seen as a problem in the past, particularly by some students who had transferred to Valley High. At Valley High some students had experienced negative interactions with Lebanese students in schools they had previously attended, and indicated that the Lebanese youth went around in groups that were intimidating. Relations between Lebanese and Black students interviewed at River High seemed less antagonistic, with one student stating that previously he had thought of Lebanon "as a terrorist place" until he met some Lebanese students.

Maintaining Boundaries

Gossip and labelling seem to be used as tools for racialized boundary maintenance. Accusations of "selling out," "whitewash" and "oreo"—of being Black on the outside but White on the inside—were taken seriously by some students. The use of racial symbols affects inter-racial relations. Roy indicated how this process of name calling works:

> Roy: *I mix with Blacks, sometimes a Brown. I usually stick with my [Black] friends.*
>
> Jennifer: *Why is that?*
>
> Roy: *It looks better. If you go somewhere and people see you, they won't label you as whitewashed. If I saw a Black guy walking with a Lebanese guy I'll be like . . . [looking]. It's better to be with your own kind.*
>
> Jennifer: *Is it a big thing to be called whitewashed?*
>
> Roy: *That hurts . . . that means you don't know about yourself.*

Ida articulated the stress associated with being seen as whitewashed and how she was able to act in spite of the name calling:

> Ida: *It's acceptable not to like White people. I don't share that belief. I guess that's why I get called whitewashed. I don't share the standards that most Black people are supposed to follow.*
>
> Jennifer: *Who calls you whitewashed?*
>
> Ida: *My friends . . . because I have White friends, and they expect me to have just Black friends . . . . They find something wrong with having White friends. I guess it's a stereotype that people have of Blacks. They have to be into sports, wear baggy clothes . . . a gang image. I don't follow that.*

Jennifer: *What does it feel like when they call you whitewashed?*

Ida: *It used to offend me but now I feel sorry for them . . . . I know I'm Black, it's not something I am choosing to be, I'm just being myself. If they can't accept it that's their problem.*

Ida's comments, although representative of a minority view, are interesting from a variety of perspectives, and indicate an anti-essentialist position. As hooks states:

> Such a critique allows us to affirm multiple Black identities, varied Black experience. It also challenges colonial imperialist paradigms of Black identity, which represent blackness one-dimensionally in ways that reinforce and sustain White supremacy. This discourse created the idea of the "primitive" and promoted the notion of an "authentic" experience seeing as "natural" those expressions of Black life that conformed to a pre-existing pattern or stereotype. (1992: 10)

Some of the students saw Blackness as being represented by specific ways of acting and by particular attitudes. During one group meeting, the students illustrated how taking part in certain leisure activities could define them as either Black or whitewashed. Sula, in defending a fellow student against charges of being whitewashed, revealed that

He is the nicest guy [but] . . . he does White things . . . going to cottages, skiing, stuff that doesn't appeal to us [Black people]. . . . He says that he doesn't like a lot of Black people in the school because they give him attitude, because he hangs out with complete White guys.

Toni: *When we see a half guy with pure White people you can't say we don't say, Ah ha, he's whitewashed!*

Sula: *It's wrong to stereotype him, if he's whitewashed, it's not our problem . . . it's his!*

Toni: *There will come a time* [said knowingly] *when the world will say he's Black. There will come a time he will have to face it.*

SUMMARY

The comments made by the students in t his study reveal how they were othered during their early school experiences and made aware of their difference from the perceived norm of White Canadian society. This experience of differentiation seemed to vary for each student according to location, age and context. It is a process that was exacerbated by the colour-blind attitude of teachers. Differentiation was reinforced in high school by an identification with others who were seen as having common experiences and understandings of "where they are coming from." Factors such as the use of patois, gossip, frequenting specific social venues, and knowledge of lived experiences in Canada and the Caribbean became intertwined with peer relations to develop and maintain racialized boundaries. This boundary maintenance was problematic, however, as students interpreted, in varying ways, what it meant to be Black. Identity was revealed as relational as the students placed themselves and other racialized groups at school within a hierarchy. Within this hierarchy differing groups were placed in differing positions. There was no one-way imposition of power from Whites to Blacks or other raced groups. Raced groups interacted with power in different ways, so that while Blacks associated Whites with having institutional power to define their school environment and life chances, they saw other raced groups such as Chinese and Vietnamese as more immediate threats in terms of their day-to-day lives. The potential and shortcomings of a collective Black identity in the wider community came to be defined in relation to societal constructions of other raced groups in multicultural Canada. The whole process is an illustration of cultural reproduction.

NOTES

1. A research report on immigrant youth conducted by Seifeddine for the Edmonton Mennonite Centre in 1994, entitled *Changing Mosaic,* indicates that, among the ethnic groups, those of African descent reported the highest level of name calling. Fifty-seven percent reported experiencing name calling "many" or "a few times."
2. Cecile Wright made similar findings concerning parents' views on racial slurs in her research into *Race Relations in the Primary School* (1992). She cites the *Swann Report* (1985: 33) as showing that the prevalence of racism was "particularly strong when [Black children] are present in relatively small numbers in school and are thus less able to be mutually supportive."
3. This hidden aspect of racism in Canada is alluded to by many authors. For example, Nourbese Philip's *Frontiers* (1992) chronicles her struggle against racism in the world of the "arts." Also see Stanley R. Barrett's (1987) work, *Is God a Racist?*
4. The "step" team was a group of students that voluntarily came together to

Georgie and Grandma Payne on the Payne farm at Wildwood, Alberta. c. 1912.

practice and perform "chorally chanted rhymes punctuated with footsteps and hand claps which set up a background of rhythm" (Gilmore 1985: 113). It was seen by the students as an alternative to traditional cheerleading teams. Performances were undertaken both inside and outside the school.

5. It's worth noting that very few of the Black students were involved in A.P programs, so this may well indicate why there are few Black students involved in the school council.

6. Individuals organize hall parties, and information about location and which sound system is playing is usually circulated via flyers. Circulation tends to be among Blacks. Some students indicated that they found them boring because, after a while, it was always the same people who came. This was often related to the small size of the Black population in Edmonton.

CHAPTER FIVE

GENDER RELATIONS

Lilieth: *It's not even anything my mom said . . . she never really says anything like that. It's just the way I was brought up, because my mom is a single mother . . . since I was young . . . and she has never had to answer to any guy . . . . A lot of guys find I have an attitude, because guys like to be in control . . . I've never had to answer to any guy [at home], so I can't take authority from guys.*

For females, "knowing where you've come from" and a sense of collective memory intertwine with patriarchal relations to both support and resist male attempts to dominate in interpersonal relations. Both males and females use stereotypes when considering how Black females and Black males act and the meaning of such actions. The stereotypes are partly constructed from the young women's interactions with significant males in their lives and partly from media images in society. A sense of collective history and knowledge about the sanctions applied to inter-racial relations also have an effect. The students' experiences reflect their Black identity, but they also reflect commonalities with other raced groups. The young Black males involved in this study, as with males in other raced and ethnic groups, apply a double standard to the issue of cross-racial dating. For example, while they to varying degrees disapprove of young Black women becoming involved in cross-racial dating, they themselves date across various raced groups.

INDEPENDENCE

Many of the young women I spoke with indicated a desire to achieve a degree of independence in their future careers. For them education was important. It was seen as a way to get accreditation that could lead to a job, which would enable them to be financially independent from men.

Alice: *I come to get my education because I want to go far in life and I don't want to depend on nobody else to support me.*

Jennifer: *What do you mean?*

Alice: *My mom always says my grandmother always said to her . . . to get a good education 'cause if your man leaves you have to support yourself and your kids . . . . It's sort of something my grandmother told my mom and my mom told me.*[1]

This theme of independence carried over into the type of occupation that the young women wanted in the future. Many of the female students described the careers that they wanted as ones in which they had autonomy.

Zora: *I don't want to work under anyone. I don't like people telling me what to do.*

Jennifer: *What do you hope for the future?*

Alice: *Starting a small business . . . I know I want to be my own boss.*

Jennifer: *Why would you like to be your own boss?*

Alice: *Again that independence thing . . . avoid confrontation that can come up with having a boss.*

Females, especially (though not exclusively) mothers and older sisters, seemed to play a role in the formation of this goal of independence. A conversation among a group of females about their mothers is illustrative:

Bev: *They always tell you, "Don't let any guy walk all over you." They sort of warn you.*

Grace: *They kind of guide you. One time I went to this guy's house and I cleaned it, and I got in trouble because my mom said don't ever be a housemaid to no guy. When you get out of school you are getting a job, and don't ever depend on a guy to take care of you . . . . At first I am like, whatever, but it's true; you realize that later.*

Maya: *That's true. I've been told that so many times . . . . Don't ever think that you are just going to marry and live off this guy always, because you don't ever know that in the future that guy will always be there. Always have something for yourself.*

This socialization by mothers was sometimes expressed non-verbally:

Lilieth: *It's not even anything my mom said . . . she never really says anything like that. It's just the way I was brought up, because my mom is a single mother . . . since I was young . . . and she has never had to answer to any guy . . . . A lot of guys find I have an attitude, because guys like to be in control . . . I've never had to answer to any guy, [at home] so I can't take authority from guys.*

The comments made by the young women are consistent with Black feminist literature, which notes that most Black girls are socialized to see themselves as needing to develop skills that enable them to be financially independent. As Dionne Brand recounts, "[E]very Black woman has a mother or grandmother who has told her that she had to do it, probably alone, and that she had to continue to find ways of surviving, that she must be cognizant that no man would rescue her" (1993: 284).

There is little evidence that suggests that young Black girls are encouraged to rely on marriage as a means of economic security (Fuller 1980; Riley 1985). Historically society has been structured so that Black males have not been in a position to take on the role of sole economic provider. Although there has been some economic improvement in this historical position and educated Black males have an increased opportunity for economic mobility, many of the young women were very aware of the advantages of establishing their potential for economic and career independence.

Relationships

Relationships between Black males and females in school were obviously affected by the differing perceptions that each gender had of their day-to-day interactions. These perceptions in turn also affected the inter-racial and cross-gender interactions in their lives. Added to this, these relations were played out against a background of racialization in wider society. Because the issues raised when discussing cross-gender interaction were often emotional and complex, forming broad generalizations from my interviews would misrepresent the viewpoints of the students and miss the variety of nuances that help us understand how race and gender interact and intersect. Perhaps, therefore, it is best to view the stories of the young Black women as echoing the differing "layers of potentiality" that can be ascribed to relationships.

Layers of potentiality refer to the various forms that a relationship can take, and the way in which it is viewed. Is it seen as long-term or short-term? How some of the young women perceived a more serious relationship with a young male was partly related to their relationships with "significant" males in their lives. As part of this process Bev described her father's impact on qualities she looked for in young Black males:

> *I was watching Oprah, and they said that most girls go for guys like their fathers, and I find that's true . . . . My dad is like a real joker, and I find that I go for people like that and he is easygoing.*

On the other hand, some of the qualities displayed by significant males are an indication of what not to look for in male partners. A decision-making process involves elimination as well as selection. Lilieth described how the general mistrust that she felt about men could be related back to her father and her brother:

> *I think that the way I look at most guys has a lot to do with my dad . . . and my brother. I look at most guys as being "dogs." My dad has ten kids; my brother is always with some . . . girl. . . . [It's the way I look at guys, it's not being done] consciously; but now [that] I think about it, I think [it's true].*

In describing the traits they were seeking in future partners, as well as the type of relationship they wanted to have with young Black men, many of the young women identified equality as important:

> Paula: *Even if the Black girl has got money we are not the type of person who will thief up two dollars and give to a guy, because they are supposed to be taking care of us. Not giving them our money . . . . Mostly we want respect . . . we don't want them to use that "B" word to us. Me and Joy always say that we would like to meet a guy who we could share things [with] . . . but right now that seems like a dream, like something that wouldn't happen—a fantasy.*[2]

Some of the young women did not want to dominate a relationship:

> Lilieth: *I seem to go for ones who are of a type . . . . I like a guy who can take care of himself. Well not take care of himself [not in a physical sense]. But I don't like a little pussy guy who I can say do this and do that. I don't like guys like that at all. I like a guy who doesn't take control of me but still controls himself.*

The subtle determining factors of who makes a potential partner for a stable long-term relationship is often a reflection of the views generated at both the macro and micro levels of society—both Black and White. At the micro level, the effect of the family on cross-racial dating emerges in the experiences of one young man:

Barrington: *[A] Black and White [relationship] would never be a happy one. She might be "down" and you might be "down" with her, but her parents will always have something to say that's mostly on the Whites' side. I was going out with this White chick and her dad told her how she should go out with people from her own race. I wasn't sweating over nothing, I just said, "O.K., cool it. Let's move on man."*

Many students indicated that their parents did not approve of dating across race differences and were even less tolerant of permanent relationships. Mothers were said to have a particularly low tolerance level, but fathers were also negative:

Jimmy: *My dad's got a big problem . . . . He doesn't want no White people in the family.*

There were some differences in the reactions to inter-racial dating where members of the family were already involved in permanent cross-racial relationships. This prior experience sometimes increased tolerance, but it could also cause problems. If a parent's previous experience of a relationship outside their own raced group was negative, then stereotyping might become reinforced.

For some of the females, having a relationship with a White young man would lead to a social existence of "limbo," as a result of being socially pressured by both Blacks and Whites. This viewpoint emerged from a female focus group:

Juliet: *There'd be stress . . . . If you go to a reggae party people would be saying "ssss" [whispering] "she's with a White man . . . Juliet come bring White man to a party." If he brings you somewhere White people are going to be "ssss" [whispering].*

Pearl: *I don't really care about [social pressure], [it's] 'cause he wouldn't know how to dance that way, [and] I'd have to speak to him in proper English every time.*

Juliet: *With a Black man they already know what you are about . . . . But with a White man, having a Black girl would be a whole different new thing . . . just like all the pressure and foolishness.*

Jennifer: *So it's partly the pressure and partly because they don't know how to behave at dances?*

Pearl: *People can say whatever the hell what they want . . . . I'll go out with who I like . . . but just the idea that they have nothing like I have . . . nothing in common.*

Lorraine: *There's no bond.*

Pearl: *Maybe in a Jamaican environment.*

Lorraine: *Maybe a White Jamaican, White Bajan, where you can talk your language even.*

Social discomfort, which arises from a perceived lack of knowledge on the part of White young men about Black experiences and lives, as well as societal reactions and potential rejection were clearly important considerations for the young women. Cross-racial dating was sure to occasion the discomfort felt by Black students when in a social setting dominated by Whites.

For many of the young Black women, a relationship with a young Black man had the "potential" of developing into something long-term, mainly because they related more to Black men than to White men as future partners. Some of the young Black men, even though they perceived Black women as potential future partners, generally did not view their present relationships as "serious." Age was likely a factor in how relationships were perceived—a trait that cut across all raced groups. Lester's remarks are probably representative of males in general, not just Black young men:

[Long-term relationships] are no good, a waste of time. When you're young you're supposed to have fun.

A few of the males who considered themselves "young" and primarily looking for "fun" in a relationship equated a relationship with young Black women at school as hard work. For these young males "hard work" was symbolized by young Black women showing "attitude" when they were approached as well as being more explicit in how they expected young men to behave in a relationship. As Barrington stated:

Black girls are always talking about how Black guys are rude . . . . All other races of girls show hospitality . . . . Black girls you talk to them and then they start fronting attitude . . . . I'm not saying that for all girls, but most. Guys like girls that are easy to approach.

Attitude

Attitude was a common descriptor used by both the young men and the young women interviewed. For young women showing an attitude was viewed as a positive form of assertion, while the young males regarded the display of women's attitude in a negative light. This difference in perception of the meaning of attitude affected the interaction between young Black males and young Black females:

> Lester: *The Black girls act like they are too bad for us . . . like they are so rough, like bitches. Girls think that they are so bad, no guy can tell them what to do. They are always getting attitude.*

When asked to explain what attitude was, most of the young women said they were seen as having an attitude because:

> Clara: *We don't stand no foolishness . . . we say what we feel, and what we think.*

Showing attitude can be seen as a form of resistance to potential male dominance in a relationship; it is a way for the young women to demand respect. For example, one young woman indicated that a show of attitude could be triggered by a young man who she did not know well putting his arm around her or calling her. She would show her annoyance by "winding" her neck and walking away. Attitude can be displayed in differing social situations. Women can use it to let a man know that he has annoyed her, or it can be used as a matter of course, as part of one's general demeanour. Some young women saw attitude as a necessary part of their interaction with Black males, as a tool for survival.

> Toni: *If you don't have an attitude, they [young men] run you down and walk all over you.*

The trigger for showing attitude seemed to be a perceived lack of respect shown by males. For many of the young women, respect was extremely important in any interaction with young men. Showing respect during an initial exchange seemed to be an important indicator of whether or not a relationship would progress. To illustrate lack of respect, one young woman described how a young man trying to attract her attention shouted, "Hey lips come over here!" She indicated that she found this extremely rude and disrespectful. This emphasis on respect is one that is echoed in Black feminist literature, and charted by Patricia Hill Collins (1991) in African American blues music and literature. Roy indicated that attitude is a trait associated with Black American women:

> Roy: *A lot of them do [have an attitude]. I think it's a way to defend themselves, but some of them take it to an extreme . . . to fit the stereotype that all Black women have to have an attitude . . . from TV shows and stuff like that.*

> Jennifer: *Is that where it comes from?*

> Roy: *I don't know . . . I associate it with that. A lot of them try to compare themselves to the American women. They think that [Black American women] have to have a lot of attitude.*

> Jennifer: *Are American women seen as having attitude?*

> Roy: *This girl was telling me if I was in the States, I'd have a lot more trouble getting Black women, 'cause they'd "diss" me left, right and centre . . . . I think it's just a stereotype that American women are so strong.*

As well as wanting women to be easy to approach and without attitude, many of the young men liked a degree of latitude in a relationship; they wanted to interact with other young women. Many felt that the Black women were "overprotective" in a relationship and "cussed them out" if they were observed talking to other young women. The narratives suggest that Black male perceptions of Black female identity have come to be affected by a dominant image in White society—the matriarch. The young men's perceptions fit with Patricia Hill Collins' descriptor of a Black matriarch as one "who emasculates Black men because she will not permit them to assume roles as Black patriarchs. She refuses to be passive and thus is stigmatized" (Collins 1990: 78).

In spite of the gender schism on inter-racial dating, there was a high degree of cohesion across gender lines when it comes to perceptions of racial dynamics in society. The young Black women showed a concern for the social and academic welfare of the young men and saw women and men as suffering the same problems of racism. This bonded the two genders.[3] Lorraine described this:

> We [young women] have people walking all over us all the time. We don't want our own men walking all over us. They should know where we are coming from. We are on the same level. We should get respect from our men even if no one else.

A few young women described how some young Black males had the potential to do well at school, but were failing or in lower streams.

> Toni: *These boys . . . have so much potential. What are [they doing with their] lives . . . . The teachers will make subliminal comments [to them].*

Other young women described the sense of alienation felt by some males and indicated that it was not easy to just tell young men who were failing to change their ways. The process of alienation had started earlier than high school and was compounded by other factors they encountered in wider society:

> Clara: *Not all Black guys growing up are so strong in their lives, they will see more hope in hoodlums running around the street than in school and education and going to university. I don't think many of them see their future as graduating at the top of their class and becoming a doctor. You can't just say Black people get into shape go to school get your act together! . . . By the time you get to high school you get so discouraged, and so tired.*

Double Standards—Inter-racial Relationships

Although the young Black males tended to choose fellow Black males as close friends, this racialized cohesion was not maintained for cross-gender relations. Some young men suggested that as a result of young Black women being assertive and "showing attitude," they were forced to have inter-racial relationships. The young Black men had relationships of varying degrees of intimacy with young women from other raced groups, but many of these young men expressed discomfort with the idea of Black women going out with men from other raced groups.[4] Many stated that while they would not physically intervene in such relationships, they might verbally indicate their displeasure.

Racialized boundary maintenance between White men and Black women was kept by young women, particularly at River High, as well as by some of the young Black men. One student recalled a situation when, as a new student, she would often chat with a young White man. After a while one of the other Black women suggested:

> Joy: *"You are attracted to too many White guys" . . . . They are not saying that I shouldn't, they are just saying that they wouldn't.*

During a focus group session the young women indicated that they were aware that at times they took part in the process of monitoring each other's behaviour. Differing perspectives emerged as to the degree to which this took place and whether or not they should be monitoring each other.

> Sula: *Sometimes we do the double standard because we say, "Oh we won't be going out with no White guy," and when we see a Black girl with a White guy, we sit and "cut her up."*

> Pearl: *I don't do that . . . . The only way I do that is if I know she is only going out with him for sex or money.*

> Lorraine: *If a White guy is going to go be dumb enough to give me money I'm going to take it.*

Perhaps part of the pressure to remain with one's raced group can be explained by Lorraine's comments that if you go with another raced group and if you have a dispute with someone within a racially mixed group then you may well be abandoned. In such circumstances a Black student may not be supported by non-Black students. One can never be sure when racialization will become an issue. The young women were generally critical of the relationships that some young Black men were having with White women. To some Black women, these relationships appeared to be based on what the young Black men could get in terms of material rewards. Some of the young women made a distinction between a relationship that was based on what one young female called "genuine attraction" and one that was based on material rewards.

> Ida: *It's not the inter-racial dating . . . it's the type of girl that they go out with . . . "wiggers." [The White girls] are forward, have preconceptions about Black men, they are going to get this from them . . . sexual . . . . Our young men don't see behind their masquerade. We being the same sex we see what they are after.*

Grace also alluded to the type of women that some Black young men choose as partners:

> *It's the fool White girls that get me mad . . . . They hold their Black man like a medallion.*

A few young women claimed that all too often the men were ashamed of their relationships and when questioned the men would indicate that it was the fault of the Black women that they went out with White women—the Black women had too much attitude. The young men described how young women from other raced groups were much more approachable.

Although class and race fragment gender constructions, at times the young Black women saw themselves as having closer ties with other non-Black women than with Black men. Ida's comments above indicate how as a young woman she felt she had a better perception of the motives of White females involved in inter-racial dating. Milton made similar comments when imputing the motives of White males involved in inter-racial relationships:

> *Black girls don't like Black guys going out with White girls. All the girls see is a White girl, they don't see what the girl is like, and the same for the guys, all they see is a White guy.*

Fewer Black females than males claimed to have had dating relationships with Whites, although some did indicate that they had non-Black male friends. Patricia Hill Collins attempts to explain why Black women might not enter into relationships with White men:

> Traditionally, freedom for Black women has meant freedom from White men, not to choose White men as lovers and friends. Black women who have willingly chosen White male friends and lovers have been severely chastised in African American communities for selling out the "race." (1990: 191)

The perspectives of some of the young men verified comments made by the young Black women about inter-racial dating. Some young men agreed that material rewards affected their choice of partners, but their explanation was that the young women from other raced groups "break them bad"[5]; they liked them to look well dressed and bought them clothing or other possessions. Desmond made a distinction between the types of young White women with whom Black males had relationships:

> *There are White girls that just hang out with Black guys 'cause it's Black guys. These are the girls that we—look at them as indecent girls. We call them "easygoing girls." You know what I mean? [But] sure there are girls that are there not because he is a Black guy but because they are a friend . . . and they've got their heads straight.*

Some of the females indicated that sex was seen by some of the young men as an important trophy in a relationship. If a young woman was not willing to oblige, men were not willing to maintain a relationship. When discussing this issue the females in both schools stressed several times that not all Black males behaved in this manner and cautioned that it was dangerous to generalize. The following gives an insightful summation of the dynamics of gender relations and the pressures that females feel at times when embarking on a relationship.

Jennifer: *Do you think that most of the relationships are about [sex]?*

Grace: *Some of them.*

Pearl: *Most of them.*

Bev: *It's not most of them, some of them.*

Grace: *Not to generalize, I think a lot of the relationships with White girls are like that. Black guys and White girls. Not all but.*

Hazel: *That's why I got dumped.*

Lilieth: *I think a lot of relationships, period, are like that because a lot of guys won't go for me, because of that. But some girls are like that too.*

Hazel: *Like, some guys [if] they get it from somewhere else, they are thinking they are going to get it from you and if you don't . . . it's "What's wrong?"*

Lilieth: *If you listen to guys talk, and if one guy says he and his girlfriend has been going out for two months and nothing, [his friend will reply,] "Nothing! If I was going out with her for a week she would have to."*

Grace: *I remember there was this guy that I liked, and we weren't really going out yet . . . and this other guy says to him, "Don't go for her, you won't get none" . . . . That's just disgusting. If that's what you are going to go out with a person for then . . . take your AIDS infected little . . . .*

This next conversation gives an idea of the views that the young men expressed and some of the factors that they saw as relating to why some young women were more compliant than others in their relationships.

Malcolm: *That's the way they can keep you. There's a lot of chicks called "gangster bitches" . . . who try to screw every Black guy in the school.*

Nelson: *In Edmonton the White girls are different, maybe they're not used to having Black guys around. In other places, some of them are "facey" like the Black girls; they don't want to buy you nothing.*

Bobby: *Some of the girls like to see their men looking good.*

Barrington: *If it's a serious [relationship], then I'll tell her that there's no need to buy me to keep me. Me and you have something going on right now.*

A number of the young men indicated that they would marry Black women, even though they might go out with non-Black women. This distinction between having a relationship with a Black woman and a White woman was illustrated by Spike:

I wouldn't fight over a White girl; that would be dumb. But if it was a Black girl, that would be a different story. If I was going out with a Black girl, and a Black guy intervened, then I might get vexed.

Among the young males in one of the crews there were expressions of wanting to have a "pure" Black child. This affected their interactions with non-Black women as Jimmy indicated:

I don't want to make the mistake of a kid, I want a full Black kid. I'm not a racist or nothing . . . I try to keep away from [White girls] . . . but if it happen it happen.

One reason given for not having children of mixed race was that they were seen as not belonging to a specific race, and were therefore subject to teasing by other "racial" groups. Another concern was the way in which, for Everton, gender affected the mixed-race experience:

I want a pure Black baby . . . 'cause guys who are half usually get cut up . . . . Except for half-caste girls who are mostly good looking . . . . Half-caste guys get called oreo.

For Melvin a problem of identity would result:

The reason I wouldn't want to have a kid with a White girl is that the kid would come up with a lot of problems . . . . It would want to know, "Am I White, am I Black, whatever?" I see it happen all the time with half-caste kids. Half-caste kids called "nigger" on the White side, "monkey" or "whitewashed" on [the] Black side.

Grace saw inter-racial relationships as having the potential to undermine a child's culture:

[Some] fool White people, they treat their [Black] kids like a medal, they have Black kids 'cause it's cool . . . . If you are going to have Black kids, you should be aware of their culture.

Gossip: Putting the Word About

The charge of "sellout" was used against young Black women who had relationships with non-Black males. It seemed that young women from Valley High participated less in this stereotyping process than did females at River High. Young women at Valley High spoke about some of the pressures they felt:

Yvonne: *Even when I was going out with a White guy, my friends in Vancouver called me a big "diss" because to them it wasn't right . . . . I thought it was different when I came up here because all the Black guys were always with White girls. And I started going out with a White guy, and my friends down there . . . said "Why are you going out with a White guy?"*

Hazel: *From my Black male friends I got "dissed," they were calling me sell-out and saying I am soft. "Why are you going out with a White guy?" . . . These two guys were asking me if I went with White guys, I said not anymore and they were saying well you are soft. And I am saying why, and they can't give me a reason. They just say that it's just different [for girls].*

Lilieth: *There is this one guy, even if he sees you talking to a White guy, he comes up to you, "Oh what are you doing checking that White guy?" You can't talk to a White guy! [Black boys] automatically think that you are checking the guy or they come down on you 'cause you are talking to a White guy, when they are there talking to a White girl.*

Insults such as "sell-out" or "whitewashed" need not be uttered verbally in order for them to work effectively. As long as all the students are aware of the actions that can bring about sanctions, then looks and gestures can effectively control social interaction. The potential sanction of social isolation also helps to maintain cohesion within the raced group. As Lorraine indicated, if a Black girl went out with a White boy on a serious basis, she would *"never be looked at by a Black male again."* Whether or not this would in fact happen was not corroborated, but the potential for such a consequence was a factor in maintaining cohesion among Black females.

Gossip also plays a role in gender relations. Some young Black men felt that a relationship between two students at school was closely monitored not only by the woman involved, but also their friends, and was susceptible to gossip.

> Nelson: *If you talk to other girls, [your girlfriend gets] mad, cause [she thinks] that you are checking the girl. Then they phone you up and cuss you out!*

> Desmond: *That's the way Black girls are; they always fight for their man.*

> Barrington: *Gossip doesn't really get outside the high school system 'cause my girlfriend isn't in high school, so I'm safe.*

> Desmond: *A lot of times high school relationships between Black guys and Black girls . . . [Black guys] try to stay away from that. Because you guys see each other everyday, you bound to get into argument because of rumour or something. So you try not to see her everyday, or every hour of the day.*

> Nelson: *True! True!*

> Desmond: *It make it worse if you are going out with a White girl in school; a lot of time the White girl expect you to be with her in a corner and your friends are watching. If you don't let it bother you, then it doesn't affect you. A lot of people get stared at; they don't want to be seen with a White girl.*

> Jennifer: *What will happen if they do?*

> Bobby: *You'll get called soft, or whitewashed.*

General gossip at school affected interactions between students. Grace related that sometimes across the general Valley High population people seem to know what a person has done before he or she has done it. The gossip would be about relationships and who likes whom or does not like whom. Everton indicated that the process of gossip was circular and could result in conflict:

> Say I say to a girl, "That guy is trying to cause trouble with me." She'll go and tell somebody and they'll tell somebody else until it gets back to that guy . . . . And that guy'll come and say, "So you think you are bad?" . . . then we end up fighting.

SUMMARY

The narratives reveal that race and gender are interlocking social relations. We see that "structures of class, racism, gender and sexuality cannot be treated as 'independent variables' because the oppression of each is inscribed within the other—is constituted by and is constituted of the other" (Brah 1992: 19).

The racist-sexist construction of Black men's sexuality is evident. Some of the young men played on these racialized constructions in order to develop a set of social relations that were beneficial to them. Language, often masculinist, was used as a mechanism and strategy to police raced boundary crossings by either gender. Although males adopted racialized gender strategies more consistently in an attempt to maintain patriarchal relations, young women used the strategy for differing reasons. While the young men were intent on maintaining freedom in their choice of dating partners, some young women used such strategies to control availability of the small numbers of Black males in the school. Young women also used these gendered-raced strategies of boundary maintenance to monitor the social relations between young Black women and other raced groups.

Although raced groups of women share a degree of unity in terms of how they are affected by patriarchal relations, their individual and collective identities are also a result of present-day and socio-historical experiences. As a result there is no "natural unity" created by biology between young women from different raced groups.

White women have historically been constructed as the "norm" in terms of beauty and marriage value in a White-dominated world. This has at times meant that Black women are perceived differently in terms of their commodity value by White men and by Black men in North American society. For example, the columns of newspapers often stress the raced characteristics necessary for a future partner, hence the demand for "Single White Females" or "Single White Males" in the personal classified advertisements of local newspapers.

Discussions between young Black men and women are a necessary part of Black women's coming to define their identity, because both Black women and men internalize the power structures that exist in mainstream society. Internally as well as externally, these structures have a real and debilitating effect on their lives because differing genders and sexualities are prey to wider societal stereotypes. Thus the way in which some of the young Black men portrayed Black women as domineering bought into the prevalent North American stereotype of the strident Black matriarch. Similarly, some of the young women had ingested stereotypes of young Black men as unreliable partners whose primary goal in a relationship was material rather than emotional.

Dating across raced boundaries was used by some as a gauge of a "true" Black identity—if you dated non-Blacks, you were not Black enough. This was particularly true for women and was policed by women as much as men. By supporting this restrictive practice, the women were subscribing to patriarchal relations in which women inhabit a subordinated position.

However, there was general resistance by many of the young women to male dominance in their social relations. But this resistance was turned back onto the young women as a reason for eliminating them as suitable short-term partners; they were depicted as having "attitude" and expecting a relationship that required "hard work."

The narratives reveal commonsense and contradictory readings of what it means to be a young Black woman or a young Black man.

NOTES

1. See, for example, Dionne Brand (1993) for similar narratives.
. This reveals a contradiction in how the girls react; even though they say they want an equal relationship, they still see males as providers.
3. bell hooks explains this process as one whereby "many Black people are just as committed to racial solidarity as White people and they believe it can best be maintained by discouraging legalized union between White men and Black women" (1981: 67).
4. Refer to hooks (1992) for an interesting discussion of reconstructing Black masculinity.
5. "Break them bad" means the women treat them too easily, spoil them. This corresponds with the analysis given by some of the young Black women.

CHAPTER SIX

Learning and Living Identity

George: *People don't understand the Black person. They don't understand Black people and their culture. They don't understand why a Black person rebels against a White person . . . like a police officer . . . . When we rebel against that they see it as . . . our fault.*

At the start of this book I outlined that one's identity is formed in relation to other social and cultural groups. Analysis of the student narratives reveals that in addition to forming an identity, students are also involved in culturally reproducing an identity of raced meanings. This process of cultural reproduction occurs at an almost unconscious level as the students come to adopt and adapt different cultural resources as representative of Blackness. Raced meanings are reproduced within a racialized Canada— a nation that is officially multicultural and colour-blind. Canada's official history reflects the ideology of the dominant group and denies racialization. Similarly, current official policy and practices deny the oppressive experiences of being Black in a White-dominated Canada.

This chapter considers the complexities of a Black identity and how the raced meanings adopted by the students come to affect how they place themselves within the classroom, the school and Canadian society. It also considers how Black identification affects the students' relationship to classroom pedagogy and the curriculum. Many teachers are unaware of the formation of a Black identity. Of those who do recognize its formation, many see it as having no effect on the way in which students experience their lives.

Racialization and Identity

Identifying oneself as Black is not solely a matter of biology. Black identity should be understood as referring to "performance," used as a verb rather than a noun, as active rather than static (Walcott 1997: 97). The experiences of the students interviewed are similar to those of their non-Black peers— they listen to music, play basketball or watch movies at the local mall. However differences emerge for those who come to identify themselves as

Black as layers of raced meanings and memories filter their experiences. These students in varying degrees draw on a historical memory of the lived experiences of Blacks in White-dominated societies in order to reflect on the present. This ability to reflect on the past has the potential to be political and cultural, as shown by those students who viewed themselves as a "group for itself." For other students Black identification stops at the cultural level of self-definition and does not require the specific promotion of Blacks as a group. Further, the identities constructed are not uniform, being dependent upon gender, religion, ethnicity, age and class. Also of importance are raced meanings and understandings that students bring from family, countries of origin and the Black Diaspora.

Thus members of Eldridge's crew drew on sources in Jamaica, the U.S. and Toronto for their dress style and other aspects of their identity, and additins of their own to develop a Black style that was similar to but different from that of their origins. In some ways this melding and merging with origins beyond Canadian boundaries is reminiscent of Paul Gilroy's concept of a Black Atlantic mentioned in the summary of Chapter Three. Referring to present-day musical forms in Britain, Gilroy attests to the importance of music in

> facilitating the transition of diverse settlers to a distinct mode of lived blackness. It was instrumental in producing a constellation of subject positions that was openly indebted for its conditions of possibility to the Caribbean, the United States and even Africa. (1993: 82)

Support of cultural forms developed from the lived experiences of Blacks, such as listening to jazz, R&B, rap and reggae, was regarded as a way of identifying with Black lived experiences. This poses the question of what can be classified as a Black art form. Are all forms of music performed by Blacks representative of Black culture? In discussing rap and reggae the issues of authenticity and appropriation of perceived Black art forms were noted. Criticisms were raised about how forms such as rap have changed when they are commodified for mass production for a non-Black audience.

Identity and Self-representation

Black bodies have become a part of the process of signifying Blackness in specific ways. Rinaldo Walcott suggests that the body "is not only used as a biological mechanism, it also works as a site for the contestation of social relations as those relations relate to acts and actions of power on and through the body" (1997: 64). It is the body as a site of contestation that is at issue in the concepts of "under the gaze" and "glaring." Here we see how the ways in which the body is dressed can become symbolic and offer opposition to the constructed norms of society. The example of being under the gaze and of glaring illustrated by Eldridge's group of males reveals not only the power of signification but also the tensions surrounding challenges to what is perceived as the norm of Canadian identity. Thus Black bodies that dress, move and walk in certain ways come to signify Other and are seen as a threat that is more than symbolic. This glaring illustrates the ability of the youths to perceive themselves as Other and then react to this in a way that moves them from an "object" perceived to a "subject" who acts.

The students displayed a Black identity that can be seen as formed along Hall's two axes of similarity and difference, which are referred to in Chapter One (Hall 1990: 226). Similarities of gender are intersected by differences of religious orientation to form one specific Black female identity. Thus one can suggest that Black identity is not "unified" but is decentred; it has a plurality of interlocking centres. In spite of this sense of fragmentation, the students still managed to maintain a unity of selves that could be identified as Black within White society.

Understandings of what Black identification means varied from student to student. The variations did not fall along straight lines of gender, race, class or religion. Thus, for example, when discussing cross-racial dating some (women and men) equated an "authentic" Black identity with dating only fellow Blacks. Any transgression of this was seen as a transgression of what it means to identify oneself as Black. For other students, such as Ida, as long as there was respect in a relationship cross-racial dating did not indicate a lesser Black self.

The youths' relationships with parents or other caregivers, and the socio-economic status of parents also affected the kind of identifications that the students could make in their lives. If the students had a strong sense of being located within their families—whereby they were influenced and closely supervised by their caregivers—then their ability to adopt identities, which required adherence to a peer group, would be curtailed. Religious organizations, such as churches, that have predominantly Black congregations offer alternatives sites of identification from the more flamboyant masculine identities offered by popular culture. For instance, the Shiloh Baptist Church in Edmonton established at the turn of the century continues to offer support to the community and youth by "ministering to the spiritual, social and physical needs of the young people" (Codjoe 1997: 429).

It is important to recognize that self-knowledge develops not just by selecting aspects of one's identity but also by differentiating the self from others. Thus an understanding and development of Black identification rests upon one's ability to recognize who one is not. Social events such as hall parties reinforce recognition of "in-groups" and "out-groups" in relation to Black identity. This level of social interaction between Black peers helps to create that differentiation from others, while at the same time reinforcing a Black identity. Further, as discussed below, the students saw few opportunities within the official school curriculum to discuss the lived experiences of Blacks in Canada or to help them understand the self in relation to White society. This lack of formal discussion meant that mixing with other Blacks was highly useful and advantageous. They turned to each other as support sites of learning.

Peers

For all youths, Black and non-Black, peer groups are a significant aspect of their school lives. Such groups generally provide important social and emotional support as students attempt to find meaning in an often alienating and competitive structure. "The peer network isn't just the place where you reinforce your image or where you communicate. It is a social structure integral to self construction" (Wexler 1992: 134). The students' narratives illustrate how, for the two crews in particular, peer networks are important in supporting a specific identification. While such peer groups engender close ties of trust, their reception by others within society and school is not so positive; they tend to be perceived as threatening. As students move to high school, friendship groups gain more racial/ethnic cohesiveness. This cohesion is also experienced in their social interaction outside of school. As within all institutions, there is a degree of overlap within school groups by individuals who do not feel the need or the pressure to adhere to one group. The ability of individual students to resist pressure to conform to a specific performance of Black identity is affected by the overall culture and climate of the school.

Friendship groups were identified by the students as important sources for gaining access to knowledge about themselves and also as sources of affective support and feedback. Particularly among the males, cliques were an evident form of grouping. This grouping may be a response to the prevalent constructions of young Black males in society as "troublemakers," which may result in their experiencing verbal and physical intimidation.

It is worth noting that while most of the media and some sociological literature portray Black working-class male group behaviour as negative, in my study the picture is more complex. For example, during my conversation with one of the crews it emerged that this group provided the basis for positive influence and informal learning:

Jennifer: *Have you got any [children]?*

Lester: *No. They call me the wisest. I tell my friends to use condoms
... I buy condoms . I give it to them. Now they all use it. I got them
into it.*

Among the male students, verbal skills as well as physical prowess
were important in gaining status in their daily interactions. Friendship
groups indicated that they spent a lot of time talking about a variety of
issues ranging from Blackness to girls to fights. The importance of verbal
skills in friendship groups was highlighted by Lynford, a member of one
of the crews:

Lynford: *We look to [Marcus] as the leader, it's not that he can
fight or anything. It's that he knows how to talk and he can get us
out of trouble when we get into trouble.*

Jennifer: *What sort of trouble?*

Lynford: *Like when we don't want to fight we'll talk our way out
of it.*

Popular Culture and Schools as Informal Sites of Learning

In terms of cultural reproduction, the youths were producing a racialized
identity using the school as one of a number of sites of formation and
learning. The importance of school for identity formation is encapsulated
by Philip Wexler:

[T]he main thing about schools is that they are one of the few
remaining public interactional spaces in which people are still
engaged with each other in the reciprocal, though organizationally
patterned labour of producing meaning—indeed the core meaning
of self identity. (1992: 10)

Generally schools produce many different raced, classed, sexed and gendered
identities as they rank and sort students using the curriculum. Similarly,
Black students use raced memories and experiences to differentiate themselves from non-Blacks. Thus the high school, by bringing students together, acts as an informal site for Black students, and others, to encounter
and learn about differing Black identifications.

"Popular culture shapes the categories of racial meaning that students
construct when interpreting their experiences, therefore prefiguring how
they produce and respond to classroom knowledge" (Haymes 1995: 106).
Television programs played a role in shaping the categories of racial

meaning that students constructed at school. Within the narratives several references were made to "Oprah" and other talk shows watched by both Black and non-Black students. In particular, programs that discussed issues related to being Black and growing up in a White-dominated society were popular themes with the students. These programs become the foci for conversations and questioning among some students as they associated themselves with, or differentiated themselves from, points expressed by various participants on these shows. Corrine Squires' research attests to the importance of "Oprah": "[T]he show has become a source of information and opinions about relationships, psychopathology and gender. It is a cultural icon, signifying at the same time lurid dilemmas, emotional intensity, fame and black women's success" (1994: 63).

Similarly, films, music videos, books, magazines and the internet provided common experiences that were analyzed by the students. Popular culture, important for all youths, therefore has a layer of raced meanings and serves as a focus for discussions of Black identity. This process of informal learning does not take the form of a static absorption of information, as is the case in some classrooms according to the students. Rather, this learning required an active learner who engaged herself or himself, posited a viewpoint and was then challenged by others.

A further important point is that most of the television programs that the students liked to watch are produced in the U.S. and generally focus on the activities of African Americans. This reveals two issues of importance that affected the ways in which the students related to each other and to the school environment. First, the students gain access to a representation of life in the U.S. even though their direct experiences are in Edmonton, which is predominantly White. Thus their vicarious experiences and the attitudes and values they are exposed to are those of U.S. society. Since race is an important construct in the U.S., the students get a "raced" dimension in their viewing, even if race is not mentioned overtly. Second, because of its predominance, the U.S. media plays a role in the construction of stereotypes such that White society comes to racialize the experiences of African Canadians based particularly on the images that reflect the lived experiences of Blacks—particularly working-class males— in the U.S. (McCarthy et al. 1997).

There are of course problems with using such sources as TV to access knowledge of the lived experiences of Blacks. Although some students equated "knowing oneself" with a "true" Black identity, this statement is problematic. Since Black identity is active and changing it is questionable whether what it means to be Black can be known once and for all. What they "know" is often a representation and can change over time. For example, heroes such as Malcolm X who were mentioned by students were often known by their media constructions, particularly by the Spike Lee film that bears Malcolm's name. While this access to media indicates a broadening of access to "knowledge" about Blacks, it also highlights the possibility that screen creations may become a primary source for gaining information. This leads to a situation that George (1992) described as youths reading things into Malcolm X but not reading Malcolm himself.

It was noticeable that the Black "hood" films watched by some of the students posited the regaining of Black masculinity and potency as the only way to save self and the community. These hood films are generally sexist in their portrayal of women whose only role is often to help the Black man save himself. As McCarthy et al. state:

> [I]n this world constructed by male film-makers, the identities of men are formed out of the ascribed negative or inferior attributes of women: "It's a boyz world they sculpt ingeniously with gunfire and gutter talk, in which the worst insult to a man is to call him a bitch." (1997: 286)

Although some youths watched films (produced primarily for a White mainstream audience) purely for entertainment, others watched with a critical eye such that this media became part of a learning process. This latter approach is espoused by Ellsworth who argues that "oppositional readings" are always possible, and it is unlikely that any individual student "will actually experience a particular film the way the film maker intended" (1993: 202). This oppositional reading draws on Black people's "collective memory" of how they have been exploited and marginalized in a White-dominated society, and recognizes the complexity of Black experiences. Memory is used as a tool of critique. The narratives of Eldridge and Nelson in Chapter Three illustrate an example of such critique. In response to White mainstream films, they remarked:

> We do stuff for ourselves but they always show the White man trying to save the Black person.

The formation of the students' Black identities takes place without most teachers having any awareness of this process. This lack of recognition of this aspect of student life is reflected in the classroom pedagogy and curriculum and also means that teachers may not be cognizant of the experiences of those students who receive and perceive their learning through their Black identity.

Some students who enter high schools have a degree of knowledge about the lives and experiences of Blacks in Canada, North America and continental Africa. For this generation of Black youths the sources of knowledge about themselves has increased along with the general explosion of televisual forms. Thus students such as Desmond recognize more readily when knowledge about the lived experiences of Blacks has been omitted from the official curriculum.

> Desmond: *Schools are so deprived of Black stuff that a social teacher who said that he had been teaching social for a long time [was surprised when] . . . I told him that the first lady in the newspaper industry was a Black lady, and he didn't know. That's something that a social studies teacher should know.*[1]

Historical Memory and Schooling

Historical memory affected the ways in which the students produce and reproduce identities and how they perceive the curriculum. This historical and collective memory maintained by parents, books, peers and other sources discussed in Chapter Three affects the way in which experiences within schools and school-produced knowledge is received. Because the dominant European group's lived experience is used to represent the "norm," the lived experiences and historical memories of African Canadians and other groups are marginalized or ignored.

This historical memory can be seen to affect aspects of schooling for African Canadian students, in particular their attitude towards racial slurs and the use of the word "nigger" in language arts texts as well as their response to the portrayal of Blacks in social studies texts.

Racial slurs such as "nigger" carry an emotional residue from the past. Parental socialization and experiences in society reinforce recognition of "nigger" as an unacceptable term. As part of living in a racialized society Black students have to learn how to deal with racial slurs. Many of the students interviewed felt that at no time was its use acceptable and that physical retaliation for use of such a slur was justifiable. Others, predominantly males, suggested that it was a term that could be used between them and other Black friends or close White friends. For a few students there was an attempt, in line with the music by rappers such as Ice Cube, for the slur to be reclaimed. This reclamation is problematic, however, because if it is used freely by Blacks then how can one prevent its general use in society?

Racial slurs are often at the root of the earliest racialized incidents experienced by Black students, and if they respond to taunting their behaviour is classified as violent. An important issue arises from incidents where racial slurs are used; some students revealed that their parents saw retaliation as a justifiable response to racial taunting. This highlights a potential conflict between students' home values and those of the school. Educators in this instance need to recognize that racial slurs often have historical and political weight behind them. They are not the same as any other terms of abuse and the aftermath of their use might require careful and sensitive handling.

LANGUAGE ARTS

The use of "nigger" in official school texts was seen by many students in this study as problematic. A lack of recognition by educators of the historical construction and the emotions a term can carry led to a situation whereby selection and use of material containing the term was based purely on rational judgement:

> Ms. Blotter: *I would appreciate it if a student says to me, "The word nigger offends me" because then I'd want to know why it offends you . . . and then we could get to the point of letting that word go . . . . It's not even a word . . . . The word niggardly exists and that means cheap . . . . It doesn't apply to a group of people with Black pigmentation. It has a social impact because we give it the power to have a social impact . . . . I am not belittling the social impact, but it's just a word.*

However, we cannot always simply rationalize students' emotions. The racist slur continues to offend the students:

> Hazel: *I didn't want to read* To Kill a Mocking Bird, *because there was too much racial tension [in the book] and being one of three Black kids in the class I felt out of place reading this thing, and [the teacher] will be reading this word "nigger" like it was no big deal.*

The students also mentioned the sensitivity of discussing issues related to race particularly when they were in a minority in a class. One of the students suggested a way around this sensitivity:

> Malcolm: *What can the teacher do to improve the atmosphere when more sensitive issues are discussed?*

> George: *Talk about the term in front of the class . . . . We did* Catcher in the Rye, *and the guy talked about "nigger" here and there. Teacher never said nothing.*

> Bryan: *Some of them do.*

> Milton: *They approach it in different ways . . . . Most of the time it makes you feel big time uncomfortable.*

If knowledge is viewed as socially constructed and open to critique, then the way in which these novels are taught could change. It might be possible therefore to move away from a focus on teaching novels about White North American experiences simply because they are regarded as "classics," and towards a position that investigates and analyzes why specific texts have become constructed as "classics." If these novels have to be studied, they should be examined critically so that students recognize the construction of racialization within them. As Toni Morrison suggests:

> [W]e need studies of the technical ways in which an Africanist character is used to limn out and enforce the invention and implication of whiteness. We need studies that analyze the strategic use of black characters to define the goals and enhance the qualities of white characters. (1993: 52)

Literature is a social product and "classics" reveal which groups have the power to have their views legitimized in the school curriculum.

As policy-makers and educators we need to recognize that youths do not come to school *tabula rasa*. They come to schools raced, gendered and classed and continue learning these constructions within their school environments. It would seem that many teachers are unaware of the raced experiences of students; for them students exist in a world in which race is of no significance. As one principal conveyed when refusing to talk to me about Black students in his school, "We like our students to think of themselves as one group." While the sentiment is laudable and fits with a colour-blind attitude, it fails to recognize the reality of racialized meanings that students encounter. As Giroux suggests, "[E]ducators need to understand and develop in their pedagogies how identities are produced differently, how they take up the narratives of the past through the stories and experiences of the present" (1993: 22).

Social Studies

Historical memory as a component of a Black cultural identity also affects the ways in which the social studies curriculum is perceived. If identity is "a narrative of the self . . . the story [that] we tell about the self in order to know who we are" (Hall 1991a: 16) then it is appropriate to ask: what stories do the students find in the official curriculum and are they the same stories that the students tell themselves?

There is a view among educators and policy-makers that social studies is the most appropriate subject area for including the lived experiences of African Canadians. Yet in general the students interviewed suggested that at present the social studies curriculum developed by Alberta Education is not one within which they would recognize the experiences of Blacks/

continental Africans. Obviously there was no uniformity as to how the students responded or the degree of critique, but illustrated below are the specifics of their disquiet.

The stories that the Black students told of themselves and their identity were filtered by and reflected on historical memory and the present-day experiences of other Blacks. These sources for identification are rooted in North America and the Caribbean in particular and in the continent of Africa historically. Most students recognized themselves as Black and referred to themselves as Black. Some used their people's collective memory to reflect on and interpret their lives, social interactions and their everyday experiences of schooling. During this process of reflection it was again evident that as part of recognizing themselves as Black they were also differentiating themselves from others:

> Maya: [Non-Blacks] always say, "Why should you guys be mad at us for what our ancestors did?"

> Grace: They are doing that same thing now only it's not as noticeable and you can't see it as easily.

> Zora: When they say that, [I say], "But we're still paying for the image that our ancestors have, we are still paying for that slavery image . . . . We are still linked to that history, but yet they want to totally forget about theirs."

The students used this sense of collective memory to filter and interpret the social studies curriculum. What their narratives reveal is a perceived lack of recognition of the intellectual contributions of Blacks, a portrayal of Blacks as one homogenous cultural group, and a lack of recognition of those of African descent as active agents in their social environment.

The Lack of Recognition of Intellectual Contribution

The students viewed Blacks as having made intellectual contributions to North American society that were not recognized in the curriculum as delivered in the classrooms. As part of this lack of intellectual recognition, some of the students I spoke with saw the curriculum as portraying Blacks as passive, as objects in their social environment:

> Desmond: I don't like the way [social studies is] taught . . . . When they talk about Africa, it's either because Africa is being invaded by another country or [about] apartheid.

> Bobby: [They] talk about Mandela; they just said that he had been

129

in prison and was now out.

Desmond: *When they talk about us in social, they talk about us being in chains. They don't talk about how we got out of it, what we did for ourselves.*

The perspective from which the curriculum was taught was also seen as implicated in this process of intellectual negation. For the students who saw their identity as Black, the colonization story told in the textbooks was very much in the language of the colonizers:

Bobby: *[They] talk about . . . all these little states in Africa, when they were founded, how the Dutch moved here-there and the French moved here-there but not before that.*

Malcolm: *[The French] invaded, but they portray . . . [them] as heroes . . .who saved these people. Nobody asked them to save us. I get pretty much pissed off.*

As part of their critique of history being viewed from the colonizers point of view, the students highlighted how representations of Africans were used as background to throw into relief the constructed benevolent qualities of the invading European groups.

Homogenization

For students such as Milton, the social experiences of Blacks discussed in the social studies curriculum were often homogenized and simplified:

Why do we have to discuss just slavery? There is a lot more . . . to Black culture than slavery.

To illustrate what this broader conception of culture entailed, students drew on the ancient civilizations of continental Africa as a source of knowledge. Some also recognized that knowledge about the intellectual contributions of Africans and Black North Americans need not be confined to the area of social studies, but could be developed across the curriculum:

Milton: *They could even mention it in mathematics, some of the things that the Egyptians did. Some of the science courses it could come up . . . . They don't need to say this is what Black people did, but they could name some people and inventions and mention that they were Black.*

In terms of their identity, there was an underlying recognition that the ways in which they were identified and represented by their peers related to the knowledge that non-Blacks had access to within the curriculum. Thus there was recognition that the curriculum had the potential to construct a one-dimensional, simplistic reading of Black experience for their fellow students. As a result all students, Black and non-Black, were gaining the impression that Black experience in Canada was modern and related solely to recent immigration from the Caribbean, rather than being rooted in Canada's past. The 1914–18 European war and the difficulties African Canadians experienced in enlisting in the Canadian Expeditionary Force is an interesting example of how school knowledge constructs "reality":

> Jennifer: *What do you think about the content of the curriculum—social studies?*
>
> Joy: *Maybe they could put a little more thing in their history. 'Cause I know a lot of Black people do good stuff. Seem like in World War whatever Blacks never take part or nothing.*

The students in both schools displayed varying degrees and depths of knowledge of Black experiences. Some of the students seemed to know of the general achievements of Black people and their contributions to mainstream society. Others had a cursory knowledge that they wanted to increase. Both cases indicate that knowledge about Blacks was inadequately represented in the curriculum. Zora made the point:

> *I did a Black history project for a showcase, and I was going to do Malcolm X, or Martin Luther King. Then my mom suggests, "Why don't you do Canadian history? Everyone hears about them [Malcolm X and Martin Luther King] but you don't know nothing about [Canadian history]." I started reading and the stuff was incredible, like Black ranchers, and Amber Valley, and golf. You think of golf as a "White man's sport," [but the] golf tee was invented by a Black person. Elevators, refrigerator. The first refrigerator was invented by a Black person, but it wasn't patented. People don't acknowledge it.*

Black students' recognition that Black experiences are not acknowledged and are often historically invisible in Canadian society challenges the myth of Canada as a consistently pluralist society. If in fact all groups are recognized within the mosaic, then why is it that we continue to suppress past involvement of Blacks and other groups—often referred to historically as the "uninvited" races—in the creation of the Canadian state (Ruttan 1998).

Most of the students interviewed would agree that multiculturalism does not recognize the Black/African in the Canadian or vice-versa. Any attempt to challenge this Eurocentric dominance is not welcomed by the mainstream of our society. Canadian society is based upon Eurocentric, individualist, liberal assumptions. When African Canadians and others who are not part of the dominant group advocate changes in the way in which school is organized, so that it becomes more inclusive in terms of structures and curriculum, their requests create tension among those upholding the dominant liberal ideology of equality. This ideology advocates that everyone should be treated the same way; the reality that differences exist between individuals, and that achieving equality might not necessarily mean that everyone is treated in exactly the same way, is ignored. For example, this tension becomes apparent when Black students or community groups request a more inclusive school environment. The liberal stress on individual rights over collective rights means that when Black-identified students ask for a more inclusive curriculum they are seen as making an unfair request and promoting the interests of Blacks above others in society. Further, because teachers do not recognize that some students come to classes with a political and social understanding of racialization, their resistance to the norms and values used to construct White dominance results in them being "labelled 'deviant' or 'problem children'" (Dei 1996: 78).

> Shaka: *Last year, I had a teacher for social, and I said let's do something about Black people and he got mad at me. And all these [classmates] were saying I hate teachers . . . and that I am a racist because I asked for a class on Black stuff.*

The recognition of dominance beyond the classroom and the reception Whites give to such recognition helps to maintain the invisibility of dominance.

> George: *I bought a book lately, it's really good; it's called* History of Slavery *. . . . I brought it to work and this girl says, "What do you need that for?" . . . "Why do you have those books . . . like* Ebony?" *"What kind of book is that?" "You don't see us with a book called* Ivory." *I says . . . what do you mean you don't have a book call* Ivory? *You have* Vogue, *you have . . . every book you have is* Ivory. *[She says] "What you talking about?" (like freaking out, like I am some sort of rebel.) I didn't want to go any further 'cause no matter what I said it wasn't going to go through her head . . . . The same thing happens in school. That's the same kind of feelings you get in class, with teachers.*

Since it is assumed that lived Black experiences are peripheral to the main curriculum, the onus for educating about Black experiences is placed firmly on the students and their families. Grace and Yvonne discussed the realities and tensions of such a position:

> Grace: *We shouldn't have to learn all our history on our own time.*

> Yvonne: *I shouldn't have to go after school to learn about my history . . . . [Whites] don't have to go after school to learn their history . . . . I remember during Black history month you were asked to do the [presentation] thing, yeah. And you couldn't.*

> Grace: *Yeah, I didn't feel that I knew enough.*

> Yvonne: *That's pretty down why do you have to learn about somebody else's culture if you are not getting a chance to learn yours?*

> Grace: *I have to go home and study and study so I can pass about someone else's culture and maybe if I have five minutes before I go to sleep I can read some other book. Last year I had so much more time to read but this year I feel as though I haven't learned anything about what I want to learn. I think it's shameful.*

The above examples of the students' views illustrate the extent of marginalization that they see and experience within the school curriculum. Over the years, although sections about individual Black persons have been added to courses, there has not been a shift in the pedagogical approach to knowledge. It is important to recognize that if we do include the lived experiences of African Canadians and other marginalized groups, and yet maintain a model of pedagogy that requires students to just absorb "facts" without questioning their construction, a position of dominance will remain. As Darder warns us, "[E]ven the most ideologically correct curriculum is in danger of objectifying students if it is utilized in such a way as to detach them from their everyday lives" (1991: 115). Therefore we should give students a voice in the construction of knowledge and reality in the classroom. Paulo Freire, the Brazilian adult educator, shows the power relations that can emerge from a teaching situation when he states:

> [P]rojecting an absolute ignorance on to others, a characteristic of the ideology of oppression, negates education and knowledge as a process of enquiry. The teacher presents himself to his student as their necessary opposite; by considering their ignorance absolute,

he justifies his own existence. (1993: 53)

Also, within the high school social studies curriculum most of the examples used relate to Europe. Even though the class might be discussing nationalism as a general concept, it is related to Germany; if the discussion is about social democratic governments, then the example studied is Sweden. This subtle European emphasis in conjunction with a focus on issues related to the European wars in 1914–1918 and 1939–45 give the overall impression that the only place where anything really important and interesting takes place is in Europe. By this critique I am not suggesting that students should not study Europe; rather, I am critiquing the presentation of European issues as universal in terms of lived experiences. I am sure that many social studies teachers see themselves as presenting a balanced and fair curriculum with references to a wide variety of geographic locations, but this may not be how some students see it:

> George: *From the White friends I have, some of them don't see themselves as White. They see themselves as French, or German, okay. What I sometimes think is it's because what they are trying to teach us in social is what society has done and try to make us see, so we can make a change. And they show us through Russia, through France, through England, through all these different countries. Maybe they see them as different nationalities but to us they are all White.*

George's comments not only highlight the invisibility of Whiteness, but also come as a reminder to those of us interested in social change that we have to view curricula holistically. As educators we need to be able to discuss the social implications of the choices we make with regard to the school-wide curriculum, so that we do not end up making the European the universal in our lessons. As Susan Edgerton argues,

> [T]he ways in which groups, individuals, and ideas come to be marginalized in a given culture, society, and/or place has much to do with what is considered to be knowledge and who is considered to possess it, who is perceived as knower and who as known. (1993: 222)

History and Canadian Multiculturalism

Connecting history and culture is also important to avoiding the portrayal of a culture as separate and having no relationship to other cultures within a society. Such separation can result in a situation where students are taught about, for example, the negative reception of the Ukranians in western

Canada without ever being told the rationale for them coming to be classified as "not of the White race." As Chapter Two's discussion of racialization reveals, Canadian society has been multicultural in the composition of its population for a long time. This is often not addressed as many prefer to maintain the myth that Canada is essentially the creation of White European races. It would be more appropriate for schooling and society to recognize this historical multiculturalism and discuss how Canada has dealt with being a multicultural society. Such a study would result in a shift away from viewing non-European immigrants in the present and focusing purely on cultural attributes such as dress, dance and diet, and a move towards actually looking at how Canada as a society has dealt with issues of "difference." Instead of focusing on racism as an American phenomenon we could come to recognize within Canadian society the ways in which "race" has been constructed and used to marginalize others. The advantage of adopting such a position is that it would move the present debates about the country and Canadian identity to a position that recognizes that differences exist and that we react and construct people in differing ways according to those differences.

In the Introduction I allude to the fact the Canada had cut the dominion umbilical cord. It now needs to start breathing on its own, it needs to start living up to its rhetoric about being a multicultural society and respecting differences. At present most students who emerge from high schools have little real political or historical understanding of how a multicultural Canada developed and how different "raced" groups contributed to the dynamic Canada that exists today. The tensions, the discriminations and the alliances analyzed in Chapter Two need to be discussed in schools.

Recognition of the construction of differences in Canadian society would affect the ways in which we undertake arguments about who is a Canadian and what rights such a citizen has to determine the present-day representations and constructions of a Canadian identity. At this point I would like to stress that I am not suggesting a simplistic equation whereby access to more knowledge about African Canadians translates into an immediate transformation in thinking. Rather, I am advocating that we try to undermine the present dominance of Eurocentrism, a "norm" that is key to the process of othering.

Conclusion

The patterns that emerge from my study reveal the mechanisms for the cultural reproduction of a Black identity. This reproduction is not uniform, nor a direct translation of the past to the present, but rather it is decentred. This Black identity—which draws on a past and present that extends beyond the boundaries of the Canadian state—has an impact on how students place themselves within their school environment. Schools are not divorced from society; they are in many ways a reflection of it. They should try to do more that just repeat and reinforce the status quo. As social race (as opposed to biological race) is a salient construct within present-day society, how individuals react to their constructions has implications for their school lives. The following comments by a teacher allude to this situation:

> Mr. Easel: *If any group of kids pick up negative stereotypes from the music from the media it's not going to reflect well on them back in school . . . . There's a lot of anger in L.A., rightly so, but a kid growing up in Edmonton doesn't have that anger, shouldn't have that anger. But it's a neat thing to be.*

Schools are sites of socialization, learning and cultural reproduction. In coming to "understand" and "know" themselves the Black students reveal that learning takes place outside the formal classroom structure as much as within its walls. The othering of Blacks in the society and institutions outside the school affect the dynamics of school life. This othering takes the form of a lack of recognition of the lived experiences of African Canadians and of stereotypes that are encountered by Black students. How the students form and reproduce Black identities is a complex task. Although there are commonalities, there is no uniformity and fixity since identities are crossed by gender, class, religion and age. As Gilroy suggests,

> Black identity is not simply a political and social category . . . it is lived as a coherent (if not always stable) sense of self. Though it is often felt to be natural and spontaneous, it remains the outcome of practical activity: language, gesture, bodily significations, desires. (1993: 102)

Students come to high school having already being "raced" in the wider society and during their elementary and junior high school experiences. Thus some of these Black students have already learned what it means to be Black in a White-dominated society. It means that you have to learn to deal with racial slurs without being categorized as violent. It means, particularly for Black males, that you have to learn that if you walk, dress and "glare" back and interrupt the "gaze" it may intimidate others. Those who feel threatened may well interpret your style as posturing and therefore open to challenge, whether physical or verbal. It means that you have to accept that knowledge and lived experiences about your ancestors and how you fit into the world will not be fully recognized by the State or by schools.

It means that you have to come to terms with the reality that others claim to know you through one-dimensional means.

Among educators there is a sense of denial that a student's race affects the way in which she or he experiences school. This seems to be based on the premise that by not acknowledging difference one is treating everyone equally. But as Toni indicated in my study:

I'm Black and I'm proud, I don't want to be grey!

Adopting a "colour-blind" attitude that does not recognize socially constructed difference does not mean that the significance of these differences disappears.

This study shows that by recognizing oneself as Black and by using peers, parents, media and community sources, one can learn what it is to be Black in a White-dominated society.

NOTE

1. The "lady" is Mary Ann Shadd, the first woman editor in North America.

References

Alexander, Ken and Avis Glaze. 1996. *Towards Freedom: The African Canadian Experience*. Toronto: Umbrella.

Alexis, Andre. 1995. "Borrowed Blackness." *This Magazine* 28(8): 14–20.

Alonso, Maria. 1988. "The Effects of Truth: Re-presentations of the Past and the Imagining of Community." *Journal of Historical Sociology* 1(1): 33–57.

Anyon, Jean. 1981. "Social Class and the Hidden Curriculum of Work." In H. Giroux, A. Penna and W. Pinar (eds.), *Curriculum and Instruction: Alternatives in Education*. California: McCutchan.

Arac, Jonathan (ed.). 1986. *Postmodernism and Politics*. Minneapolis: University of Minnesota Press.

Bannerji, Himani (ed.). 1995. *Returning the Gaze: Essays on Racism, Feminism and Politics*. Toronto: Sister Vision.

Banton, Michael. 1977. *The Idea of Race*. London: Tavistock.

_____. 1967. *Race Relations*. London: Tavistock.

Barker, Martin. 1981. *The New Racism*. London: Junction.

Barrett, Stanley. 1987. *Is God a Racist? The Right Wing in Canada*. Toronto: University of Toronto Press.

Bedggodd, D. 1980. *Rich and Poor in New Zealand*. Auckland: Allen.

Bhabha, Homi. 1990. "The Third Space." In J. Rutherford (ed.), *Identity, Community, Culture, and Difference*. London: Lawrence and Wishart.

Billig, Michael. 1995. *Banal Nationalism*. London: Sage.

_____. 1982. *Ideology and Social Psychology*. Oxford: Blackwell.

Bissoondath, Neil. 1994. *Selling Illusions: The Cult of Multiculturalism*. Toronto: Penguin.

Black Learners Advisory Committee (BLAC). 1994. *Black Report of Education: Redressing Inequity: Empowering Black Learners (Volume 1: Summary)*. Halifax: Black Learners Committee.

Blumer, H. and T. Duster. 1980. "Theories of Race and Social Action." In *Sociological Theories: Race and Colonialism*. Paris: UNESCO.

Boyko, John. 1995. *Last Step to Freedom: The Evolution of Canadian Racism*. Winnipeg: Watson and Dwyer.

Brah, Atvar. 1992. "Difference Diversity and Differentiation." In James Donald and Ali Rattansi (eds.), *"Race," Culture and Difference*. London: Sage.

Brand, Dionne. 1993. "A Working Paper on Black Women in Toronto: Gender, Race and Class." In Himani Bannerji (ed.), *Returning the Gaze: Essays on Racism, Feminism and Politics*. Toronto: Sister Vision.

_____. 1991. *No Burden to Carry: Narratives of Black Working Women in Ontario, 1920s to 1950s*. Toronto: Women's Press.

Bristow, Peggy, Dionne Brand, Linda Carty, Aufa Cooper, Sylvia Hamilton and Adrienne Shadd. 1994. *We're Rooted Here and They Can't Pull Us Up: Essays in African Canadian Women's History*. Toronto: University of Toronto Press.

Britzman, Deborah. 1991. "Decentering Discourses in Teacher Education: Or, the Unleashing of Unpopular Things." *Journal of Education* 173(3): 60–80.

Calliste, Agnes. 1993/94. "Race, Gender and Canadian Immigration Policy: Blacks from the Caribbean, 1900–1932." *Journal of Canadian Studies* 28(4): 131–48.

Carby, Hazel. 1982. "White Women Listen! Black Feminism and the Boundaries of Sisterhood." In Centre for Contemporary Cultural Studies (eds.), *The Empire Strikes Back*. Birmingham: Hutchinson.

Carroll, Jean. 1994. "The Return of the White Negro." *Esquire* 121(6): 100–07.

Carter, Velma and Wanda Akili. 1981. *The Window of Our Memories*. St. Albert: B.C.R. Society of Alberta.

Chalmers, Virginia. 1997. "White Out: Multicultural Performances in a Progressive School." In Michelle Fine, Lois Weis, Linda Powell and L. Mun Wong (eds.), *Off White: Readings on Race, Power, and Society*. New York: Routledge.

Codjoe, Henry. 1997. *Black Students and School Success*. Doctoral thesis, University of Alberta, Edmonton.

Collins, H. Patricia. 1991. *Black Feminist Thought: Knowledge, Consciousness and the Politics of Empowerment*. New York: Unwin Hyman.

Conrad, Margaret, A. Finkel and C. Jaenen. 1993. *History of the Canadian Peoples. Vol II. 1867 to the Present*. Toronto: Copp Clark.

Cooke, Britton. 1911. "The Black Canadians." *Maclean's* 23(1): 3–11.

Cooper, Afua. 1991. *Black Teachers in Canada West, 1850–1870: A History*. Masters thesis, University of Toronto.

Darder, Antonia. 1991. *Culture and Power in the Classroom: A Critical Foundation for Bicultural Education*. New York: Bergin and Garvey.

de Lepervanche, Maria and Gillian Bottomley (eds.). 1988. *The Cultural Construction of Race*. Sydney: Sydney Association for Studies in Society and Culture.

Dei, George. 1996. *Anti-Racism Education: Theory and Practice*. Halifax: Fernwood.

Department of Education and Science (DES). 1985. "Education for All." *Swann Report*. London: HMSO.

Dyer, Richard. 1988. "White." *Screen* 29(4): 44–65.

Dyson, Michael. 1993. "Be Like Mike? Michael Jordan and the Pedagogy of Desire." *Cultural Studies* 7(1): 64–72.

Easthope, Antony and Kate McGowan (eds.). 1992. *A Critical and Cultural Theory Reader*. Toronto: University of Toronto Press.

Edgerton, Susan. 1993. "Toni Morrison: Teaching the Interminable." In C. McCarthy and W. Crichlow (eds.), *Race Identity and Representation in Education*. London: Routledge.

Edmonton Journal. 1994. "Oprah Winfrey Talks Viewers Listen." July 16: B2.

Edmonton Social Planning Council. 1992. *Because of Colour*. Edmonton: Edmonton Social Planning Council.

Elliott, Jean and Augie Fleras. 1992. *Unequal Relations: An Introduction to Ethnic and Racial Dynamics in Canada*. Scarborough: Prentice.

Ellsworth, Elizabeth. 1993. "I Pledge Allegiance: The Politics of Reading and Using Educational Films." In C. McCarthy and W. Crichlow (eds.), *Race Identity and Representation in Education*. London: Routledge.

Fanon, Frantz. 1967. *Black Skins White Masks*. New York: Grove Cross.

Farquharson, Duart. 1994. "Cartoonist with an Empathetic Message." *Edmonton Journal,* June 26: A7.

Fields, Barbara. 1990. "Slavery, Race, and Ideology in the United States of America." *New Left Review* 181: 95–118.

Figueroa, Peter. 1991. *Education and the Social COnstruction of 'Race'*. London: Routledge.

Fine, Sean. 1992. "Employment." *Globe and Mail*. December 30:A1.

Finkel, Alvin, Margaret Conrad and Veronica Strong-Boag. 1993. *History of the Canadian Peoples Vol. II, 1867 to the Present*. Toronto: Copp Clark.

Foster, Cecil. 1996. *A Place Called Heaven: The Meaning of Being Black in Canada*. Toronto: Harper Collins.

Foucault, Michel. 1980. *Power/Knowledge: Selected Interviews and Other Writings 1972–1977*. Ed. Colin Gordon. New York: Pantheon.

Frankenberg, Ruth. 1993. *White Women Race Matters: The Social Construction of Whiteness*. Minneapolis: University of Minnesota Press.

Fuller, Margaret. 1980. "Black Girls in a London Comprehensive." In R. Deem (ed.), *Schooling for Women's Work*. London: Routledge and Kegan Paul.

Freire, Paulo. 1993. *Pedagogy of the Oppressed*. New York: Continuum.

George, Nelson. 1992. *Buppies, B-boys, Baps, Bohos: Notes on Post-soul Black Culture*. New York: Harper Collins.

Gilmore, Peggy. 1985. "Gimme Room: School Resistance, Attitude and Access to Literacy." *Journal of Education* 167(1): 111–28.

Gilroy, Paul. 1993. *The Black Atlantic*. Cambridge: Harvard University Press.

_____. 1991. *There Ain't No Black in the Union Jack*. London: Hutchinson.

Giroux, Henry. 1996. *Fugitive Cultures: Race, Violence and Youth*. New York: Routledge.

_____. 1993. "Living Dangerously: Identity Politics and the New Cultural Racism: Towards a Critical Pedagogy of Representation." *Cultural Studies* 7(1): 1–27.

Giroux, Henry and David Trend. 1992. "Cultural Workers, Pedagogy and the Politics of Difference: Beyond Cultural Conservatism." *Cultural Studies* 6(1): 51–71.

Goetz, Judith and Margaret LeCompte. 1984. *Ethnography and Qualitative Design in Educational Research*. California: Academic.

Gordon, M. 1964. *Assimilation in American Life*. New York: Oxford University Press.

Grange, Michael. 1995. "Students Ignorant of Canada's Racist Past, Survey Indicates." *Globe and Mail*, September 25: A3.

Gray, Herman. 1993. "African-American Political Desire and the Seductions of Contemporary Cultural Politics." *Cultural Studies* 7(3): 364–73.

Hall, Stuart. 1993. "Culture, Community, Nation." *Cultural Studies* 7(3): 349–63.

_____. 1992. "The Question of Cultural Identity." In S. Hall, D. Held and T. McGrew (eds.), *Modernity and Its Futures*. Milton Keynes: Open University Press.

_____. 1991a. "Ethnicity: Identity and Difference." *Radical America* 23(4): 9–20.

_____. 1991b. "The Local and the Global: Globalization and Ethnicity." In A. King (ed.), *Culture, Globalization and the World-System*. London: Macmillan.

_____. 1990. "Cultural Identity and Diaspora." In J. Rutherford (ed.), *Identity Community, Culture, and Difference*. London: Lawrence and Wishart.

Harris, Herbert. 1995. "Introduction: A Conceptual Overview of Race, Ethnicity, and Identity." In Herbert Harris, Howard Blue and Ezra Griffith, *Racial and Ethnic Identity: Psychological Development and Creative Expression*. New York: Routledge.

Harris Herbert, Howard Blue and Ezra Griffith (eds.). 1995. *Racial and Ethnic Identity: Psychological Development and Creative Expression*. New York: Routledge.

Hartley, John. 1994. "Representation." In Tim O'Sullivan, John Hartley, Danny Saunders, Martin Montgomery and John Fiske (eds.), *Key Concepts in Communication and Cultural Studies*. 2nd. ed. London: Routledge.

Haymes, Stephen N. 1995. "White Culture and the Politics of Racial Difference: Implications for Multiculturalism." In C. Sleeter and P. McLaren (eds.), *Multicultural*

Education, Critical Pedagogy and the Politics of Difference. New York: SUNY.

Hebdige, Dick. 1987. *Cut' n' Mix: Culture, Identity and Caribbean Music.* London: Methuen.

_____. 1979. *Subculture: The Meaning of Style.* London: Methuen.

Henry, Frances and Carol Tator. 1994. "Ideology of Racism: Democratic Racism." *Canadian Ethnic Studies* 26(2): 1–14.

hooks, bell. 1994. *Teaching to Transgress: Education as the Practice of Freedom.* London: Routledge.

_____. 1992. *Black Looks.* Toronto: Between the Lines.

_____. 1989. *Talking Back.* Boston: South End.

_____. 1984. *Feminist Theory: Margin to Centre.* Boston: South End.

_____. 1981. *Ain't I a Woman?* Boston: South End.

Hooks, Gwen. 1997. *The Keystone Legacy: Reflections of a Black Settler.* Edmonton: Brightest Pebble.

Hudak, Glenn. 1993. "Technologies of Marginality." In C. McCarthy and W. Crichlow (eds.), *Race, Identity and Representation in Education.* New York: Routledge.

Jackson. Philip. 1968. *Life in Classrooms.* New York: Holt.

James, Carl. 1990. *Making It: Black Youth, Racism and Career Aspirations in a Big City.* Oakville: Mosaic.

Killan, Crawford. 1978. *Go Do Some Great Things: The Black Pioneers of British Columbia.* Vancouver: Douglas and McIntyre.

Kluckhohn, C. 1949. *Mirror for Man: The Relation of Anthropology to Modern Life.* New York: Whittlesay House.

Kostash, Myrna. 1977. *All of Baba's Children.* Edmonton: Hurtig.

Koza, Julia. E. 1994. "Rap Music: The Cultural Politics of Official Representation." *The Review of Education /Pedagogy/Cultural Studies* 16(2): 171–96.

Labov, William. 1973. "The Logic of Nonstandard English." In N. Keddie (ed.), *Tinker Tailor: The Myth of Cultural Deprivation.* Harmondsworth: Penguin.

Lather, Patti. 1991. *Getting Smart: Feminist Research and Pedagogy With/in the Postmodern.* New York: Routledge.

Lechte, John. 1988. "Ethnocentrism, Racism, Genocide." In M. de Lepervanche and G. Bottomley (eds.), *The Cultural Construction of Race.* Sydney: Sydney Association for Studies in Society and Culture.

LeCompte, Margaret. 1978. "Learning to Work: The Hidden Curriculum of the Classroom." *Anthropology and Education Quarterly* 9(1): 22–37.

Levi-Strauss, Claude. 1966. *The Savage Mind.* London: Weidenfeld and Nicolson.

Levinson, Bradley. 1992. "Ogbu's Anthropology and the Critical Ethnography of Education: A Reciprocal Interrogation." *Qualitative Studies in Education* 5(3): 202–25.

Mason, David. 1986. "Controversies and Continuities in Race and Ethnic Relations." In J. Rex and D. Mason (eds.), *Theories of Race and Ethnic Relations.* Cambridge: Cambridge University Press.

McCarthy, Cameron and Warren Crichlow (eds.). 1993. *Race Identity and Representation in Education.* New York: Routledge.

McCarthy, C. A., Rodriguez, E. Buendia, S. Meacham, S. David, H. Godina, K. Supriya and C. Wilson-Brown. 1997. "Danger in the Safety Zone: Notes on Race, Resentment, and the Discourse of Crime, Violence and Suburban Security." *Cultural Studies* 11(2): 274–95.

McClintock, A. 1994. "Soft-soaping Empire: Commodity Racism and Imperial Advertising." In George Robertson, Melinda Mash, Lisa Tickner, Jon Bird, Barry Curtis and Tim Putnam (eds.), *Travellers' Tales: Narratives of Home and Displacement.* London: Routledge.

McLaren, Peter. 1993. "Multiculturalism and the Postmodern Critique: Towards a Pedagogy of Resistance and Transformation." *Cultural Studies* 7(1): 118–46.

Mead, George H. 1934. *Mind, Self, and Society.* Chicago: University of Chicago Press.

Miles, Robert. 1988. "Beyond the 'Race' Concept: The Reproduction of Racism in England." In M. de Lepervanche and G. Bottomley (eds.), *The Cultural Construction of Race.* Sydney: Sydney Association for Studies in Society and Culture.

_____. 1982. *Racism and Migrant Labour.* London: Routledge and Kegan Paul.

Miles, Robert and Anne Phizacklea. 1977. "Class, Race, Ethnicity and Political Action." *Political Studies* 25(4): 491–507.

Mitchell, Alanna. 1998. "Face of Big Cities Changing." *Globe and Mail,* February 18: A1.

Montague, A. 1974. *Man's Most Dangerous Myth: The Fallacy of Race.* 5th ed. New York: Oxford University Press.

Morgan, David. L. 1988. *Focus Group as Qualitative Research.* Newbury Park, CA: Sage.

Morrison, Toni. 1993. *Playing in the Dark.* New York: Vintage.

Mullard, Chris. 1986. "Pluralism, Ethnicism and Ideology: Implications for a Transformative Pedagogy." Publication Series, Working Paper no 2. Amsterdam: Centre for Race and Ethnic Studies (CRES).

Multicultural Leaders. 1993. *Working Sub-Committee Report on Discrimination in Schools.* Edmonton: Alberta.

Newman, W. 1973. *American Pluralism: A Study of Minority Groups and Social Theory.* New York: Harper and Row.

Ng, Roxana. 1993. "Sexism, Racism, Canadian Nationalism." In Himani Bannerji, (ed.), *Returning the Gaze: Essays on Racism, Feminism and Politics.* Toronto: Sister Vision.

Njeri, Itabari. 1993. "Untangling the Roots of the Violence Around Us—On Screen and Off." *Los Angeles Times Magazine,* August 29:34.

O'Farrell, Clare. 1989. *Foucault: Historian or Philosopher.* Hampshire: Macmillan.

Ogbu, John. 1992. "Understanding Cultural Diversity and Learning." *Educational Researcher* 21(8): 5–14.

Omi, Michael. 1989. "In Living Colour: Race and American Culture." In Ian Angus and Sut Jhally (eds.), *Cultural Politics in Contemporary America.* New York: Routledge.

Omi, Michael and H. Winant. 1993. "On the Theoretical Concept of Race." In C. McCarthy and W. Crichlow (eds.), *Race Identity and Representation in Education.* New York: Routledge.

_____. 1986. *Racial Formation in the United States: From 1960s to 1980s.* New York: Routledge.

Palmer, Howard. 1975. *Immigration and the Rise of Multiculturalism.* Toronto: Copp Clark.

Palmer, Howard and Tamara Palmer. 1981. "Urban Blacks in Alberta." *Alberta History* 29(3): 8–18.

Peck, Janet. 1994. "Talk about Racism: Framing a Popular Discourse of Race on Oprah Winfrey." *Cultural Critique* 27: 89–126.

Pieterse, Jan Nederveen. 1992. *White on Black: Images of Africa and Blacks in Western*

Popular Culture. New Haven: Yale University Press.

Philip, M. Nourbese. 1992. *Frontiers: Essays and Writings on Racism and Culture.* Ontario: Mercury.

Philp, Margaret. 1988. "Census Data Reveal Lag in Visible-Minority Hiring." *Globe and Mail,* February 18: A3.

Pilton, James. 1951. *Negro Settlement in British Columbia.* Masters Thesis. University of British Columbia.

Pollock, G. 1994. "Territories of Desire: Reconsiderations of an African Childhood." In G. Robertson et al. (eds.), *Travellers' Tales: Narratives of Home and Displacement.* London: Routledge.

Porter, John. 1965. *The Vertical Mosaic: An Analysis of Social Class and Power in Canada.* Toronto: University of Toronto Press.

Pryce, Ken. 1979. *Endless Pressure: A Study of West Indian Life-Styles in Bristol.* Middlesex: Penguin.

Riley, K. 1985. "Black Girls Speak for Themselves." In G. Weiner (ed.), *Just a Bunch of Girls:* Feminist Approaches to Schooling. Milton Keynes: Open University Press.

Rist, Ray. 1970. "Student Social Class and Teacher Expectations: The Self-Fulfilling Prophecy in Ghetto Education." *Harvard Education Review* 40(3): 411–51.

Rosenthal, R. and L. Jacobson. 1968. *Pygmalion in the Classroom.* New York: Holt.

Ruck, Calvin. 1987. *The Black Battalion: 1916–1920 Canada's Best Kept Military Secret.* Halifax: Nimbus.

Ruttan, Susan. 1998. "Black Only One Colour of Alberta's 'Rainbow.'" *Edmonton Journal,* February 14: I2.

Sarup, Madan. 1991. *Education and the Ideology of Racism.* Stoke-on-Trent: Trentham.

Schick, Carol. 1995. "Racial Formation in the Reporting of Canadian Immigration Figures." *36th Annual Adult Education Research Conference.* Edmonton: Department of Educational Policy Studies, University of Alberta.

Seifeddine, S. 1994. *Changing Mosaic: A Needs Assessment of Immigrant Youth in Edmonton.* Edmonton: Mennonite Centre for Newcomers.

Shadd, Adrienne. 1991. "Institutionalized Racism and Canadian History" In O. McKague (ed.), *Racism in Canada.* Saskatchewan: Fifth House.

Shepard, R. Bruce. 1991. "Plain Racism: The Reaction Against Oklahoma Black Immigration to the Canadian Plains." In O. McKague (ed.), *Racism in Canada.* Saskatchewan: Fifth House.

_____. 1976. *Black Migration as a Response to Repression: The Background Factors and Migration of Oklahoma Blacks to Western Canada 1905–1912, As a Case Study.* Masters thesis. Saskatoon: University of Saskatchewan.

Simon, Roger. 1987. "Being Ethnic/Doing Ethnicity: A Response to Corrigan." In Jon Young (ed.), *Breaking the Mosaic: Ethnic Identities in Canadian Schooling.* Toronto: Garamond.

Smith, David. 1986. "Pluralism, Race and Ethnicity in Selected Countries." In J. Rex and D. Mason (eds.), *Theories of Race and Ethnic Relations.* Cambridge: Cambridge University Press.

Solomon, Patrick. 1994. "Academic Disengagement: Black Youth and the Sports Subculture from a Cross-National Perspective." In Lorna Erwin and David MacLennan (eds.), *Sociology of Education in Canada: Critical Perspectives on Theory, Research and Practice.* Toronto: Copp Clark Longman.

_____. 1992. *Black Resistance in High School: Forging a Separatist Culture*. New York: SUNY.

Spivak, Gayatri. 1993. *Outside in the Teaching Machine*. New York: Routledge.

Squires, Corinne. 1994. "Empowering Women? The Oprah Winfrey Show." In K-K. Bhavnani and A. Phoenix (eds.), *Shifting Identities, Shifting Racisms*. London: Sage.

Statistics Canada. 1996. *Census Dictionary*. Ottawa: Industry Canada, 1977–1996 Census of Canada. Cat. no. 92-351-XPE.

Thakur, Andra. 1988. *The Impact of Schooling on Visible Minorities: A Case Study of Black Students in Alberta Secondary School*. Nanaimo: Malaspina College.

Thomas, W. and D.S. Thomas. 1928. *The Child in America: Behaviour Problems and Programs*. New York: Knopf.

Thomson, Colin. 1979. *Blacks in Deep Snow: Black Pioneers in Canada*. Ontario: Dent.

Torczyner, James. 1997. *Diversity, Mobility, and Change: The Dynamics of Black Communities in Canada*. Montreal: McGill Consortium for Ethnicity and Strategic Social Planning.

Troper, Harold. 1972."The Creek-Negroes of Oklahoma and Canadian Immigration, 1909–11." *Canadian Historical Review* 53(3): 272–88.

Tulloch, Headley. 1975. *Black Canadians*. Toronto: New Canada.

van den Berghe, Peter. 1983. "Class Race and Ethnicity in Africa." *Ethnic and Racial Studies* 6(April): 221–36.

Walcott, Rinaldo. 1997. *Black Like Who?* Toronto: Insomniac.

Walker, James. 1989. "Race and Recruitment in World War I: Enlistment of Visible Minorities in the Canadian Expeditionary Force." *Canadian Historical Review* 70(1): 1–26.

_____. 1980. *A History of Blacks in Canada*. Ottawa: Supply and Services.

Wallace, Michelle. 1990. *Invisibility Blues*. New York: Verso.

Wallerstein, Immanuel. 1991. "The Construction of Peoplehood: Racism Nationalism, Ethnicity." In E. Balibar and I. Wallerstein (eds.), *Race, Nation, Class*. London: Verso.

Werner, O. and M.G. Schoepfle. 1987. *Systematic Fieldwork Vol. 2, Ethnographic Analysis and Data Management*. Newbury Park, CA: Sage.

West, Cornel. 1993. "New Cultural Politics" In C. McCarthy and W. Crichlow (eds.), *Race Identity and Representation in Education*. New York: Routledge.

Wetherall, Margaret and Jonathan Potter (eds.). 1992. *Mapping the Language of Racism*. New York: Columbia.

Wexler, Philip. 1992. *Becoming Somebody: Toward a Social Psychology of School*. London: Falmer.

Willis, Paul. 1977. *Learning to Labour*. Farnborough, UK: Saxon House.

Winks, Robin. 1971. *The Blacks in Canada*. New Haven: Yale University Press.

_____. 1969. "Negro School Segregation." *Canadian Historical Review* 50(2): 164–91.

_____. 1968. "The Canadian Negro: A Historical Assessment." *The Journal of Negro History* 53(4): 283–300.

Wright, Cecile. 1992. *Race Relations in the Primary School*. London: David Fulton.

Yinger, John M. 1986. "Intersecting Strands in the Theorization of Race and Ethnic Relations." In J. Rex and D. Mason (eds.), *Theories of Race and Ethnic Relations*. Cambridge: Cambridge University Press.